IN MEMORY OF

HAL LEONARD III

from

W. BRUCE SAMPLES

1998

Women
Business Leaders

Women Business Leaders

Robert B. Pile

Foreword by Rose Totino

The Oliver Press, Inc.
Minneapolis

Library of Congress Cataloging-in-Publication Data

Pile, Robert B., 1918-
Women business leaders / Robert B. Pile : foreword by Rose Totino.
p.   cm— (Profiles)
Includes bibliographical references and index.
Summary: Profiles eight successful women entrepreneurs engaged in a variety of enterprises, including Mary Kay Ash, Marilyn Hamilton, Louise Woerner, Ellen Terry, Leeann Chin, Helen Boehm, Ella Musolino, and Masako Boissonnault.
ISBN: 1-881508-24-2
1. Women executives—United States—Biography—Juvenile literature. 2. Women in business—United States—Biography—Juvenile literature. [1. Businesswomen. 2. Executives. 3. Women—Biography.] I. Title. II. Series: Profiles (Minneapolis, Minn.)
HD6054.4.U6P55 1995
658.4'0092'273—dc20
[B]   94-46814
                                                             CIP
                                                             AC

ISBN: 1-881508-24-2
Profiles XIX
Printed in the United States of America

99 98 97 96 95   8 7 6 5 4 3 2 1

Dedication

The dictionary tells us that an entrepreneur is one who organizes, manages, and assumes the risks of business. True, but it doesn't come close to telling us what an entrepreneur really is.

In today's world of specialists, the entrepreneur has to be a generalist—good at many different things. On a given day, an entrepreneur may be involved in literally hundreds of different details, moving from one problem to another . . . facing opportunity here, and total failure there. Within an hour, he or she make take a risk that could bring down the company, and all employees would lose their jobs. Or, on the other hand, a right decision could move the business on to some glorious success.

Not very many people really understand the entrepreneur. There are relatively few of them, and we may never get to know one well. If we did, we'd find, of course, that they're flesh and blood, as we are. They laugh and cry as we do.

But they also do this: they start the engine, they make the wheels move and the balls bounce, they build the tall buildings, they publish the books. They give employment to millions. They stir the spirit. They make our country go.

Here's to them.

Contents

After receiving numerous compliments on her pizza, Rose Totino opened her own business in 1951. In 1975, the successful entrepreneur sold her business, Totino's Italian Kitchen, to The Pillsbury Company.

Foreword

*T*his book is about eight women who have started successful businesses in the United States. Because I am a woman, and because I, too, helped to build a business many years ago, I especially want you to read and appreciate the stories of the women in this book.

Throughout most of U.S. history, women experienced great difficulties when they tried to succeed in the business world. Society still preferred that they stay at home, clean the house, cook the meals, and raise the children. But as the years passed, some women began to work outside the home. In many cases, their families needed the extra money. In other situations, these women found work outside the home because they believed they had talents and skills that would allow them to be successful in the business world.

As you read about the eight women featured in this book, you will find that every one of them overcame serious obstacles on her way to achieving success. No one handed them anything; for the most part, they succeeded on their own. What I hope you will learn about these eight women is that each of them has two qualities in common: determination and faith.

My own parents were Italian immigrants. Our family had little money, but we loved each other and had a strong faith in God. Early in my life, I learned to cook, and pretty soon I could create a special kind of Italian dish called "pizza pie." My friends thought these pies were delicious, and they encouraged me to start selling my own pizza. Over the years, my company became a thriving business.

I hope that when you finish this book, you will understand that you, too, can achieve success in business, if that is what you wish to do. But success does not come easily. You must work to achieve success. All of us can be successful if we dare to try and if we have real faith—faith in ourselves, faith in other human beings, and faith in God.

—Rose Totino
Vice-President,
The Pillsbury Company

Author's Note

*A*s I began work on this book, I asked Rose Totino if she would write the foreword, and she graciously accepted. I had gotten to know Rose Totino while writing her story in *Top Entrepreneurs and Their Businesses*, my first book about business leaders. She was among the most gracious and delightful people I have ever known. She was an entrepreneur, but she was more than that, she was a simply magnificent human being.

While writing the last few chapters of this book, I learned that Rose was ill with cancer. Before her death on June 21, 1994, her two daughters gave me permission to include her foreword. I am deeply grateful to them, and also to Deanna Hulme, her longtime secretary at The Pillsbury Company.

—*Robert B. Pile*
Minneapolis, 1995

Acknowledgements

Several of the entrepreneurs featured in this book helped me with my research. Masako Boissonnault answered my letters and sent me photos to illustrate her story. So did Louise Woerner and Marilyn Hamilton. One of Helen Boehm's assistants sent me valuable information about the porcelain business and the Boehm Studio, and one of Ella Musolino-Alber's assistants also helped me.

Ellen Terry's mother located several photos of her daughter for me. Randall Oxford, a vice president at Halcyon Associates in Dallas, Texas, supplied me with information about Mary Kay Ash. I interviewed Leeann Chin about her great success in the restaurant business in Minnesota. Also helpful with Leeann's story was one of her assistants, Dori Karillo, as well as the Minneapolis public relations firm of P. Lindquist & Associates.

While working on the book, I read everything I could about these women. As I did, a curious and wonderful thing happened. I felt as if I were sitting in their offices or homes—interviewing them, chatting with them, living their business experience with them. I identified with their problems and understood the difficulties they experienced as they started and built their companies. But I also cheered when I learned how they had beaten the odds and achieved success.

Writing a book can be hard work, but it is also fun to see a story take shape and come alive. Part of the excitement comes from getting to know the people I'm writing about. Each of them took the time to help me and see that I got the information necessary to write the best possible story. Each of them also saw to it that I got the photos I asked for to make each chapter more real and interesting. To all of these people, I owe considerably more than a simple "thank you."

—*Robert B. Pile*
Minneapolis, 1995

HOME ECONOMICS

This illustration from around 1930 reflected the widely held belief of the day that a woman's place of "business" was in the home and, specifically, in the kitchen.

Introduction

*T*hroughout most of history, people could not even imagine that a woman might start her own business. Although women were working as shopkeepers as early as 1850, most people thought that women should work only in the home, and many believed that women lacked the shrewdness and the courage that was necessary to be successful in business.

But times have changed over the years. When many men went to fight overseas during World War I, more than 1.5 million women temporarily took over manufacturing, clerical, and service jobs that had once been held by men. By the early 1920s, more than 8 million women were a part of the U.S. work force. During World War II, women again filled the jobs held by men who went off to

In 1920, two years after the end of World War I, the Nineteenth Amendment gave American women the right to vote. The great contributions women made toward the war effort had helped them to gain equal political status with men, and represented a large step down the long road to economic equality as well.

war—but it would take many more years before some Americans would accept women in the work force.

Today, thousands of women run their own companies. Although most of these businesses are not large, employing perhaps only a handful of people and showing only a small profit each year, several U.S. women have turned their small businesses into large companies. (Experts say that only one percent of businesses owned by women have yearly profits of more than $100,000.)

The eight women profiled in this book have proved that women can indeed succeed in the challenging world of business. Mary Kay Ash is the founder of one of the best known businesses in the United States. Today, more than 375,000 sales consultants distribute Mary Kay Cosmetics. Ellen Terry's realty company in Dallas, Texas, is considered to be one of the finest real-estate businesses in the nation, and Minnesota restaurateur Leeann Chin's cookbooks have sold nearly one-half million copies throughout the world.

Although Helen Boehm's business began in a small studio in Trenton, New Jersey, the thriving company has become a supplier of porcelain figures to U.S. presidents and world leaders. Masako Boissonnault's Los Angeles interior design firm, ARCHI-FORM, has designed and decorated offices for national hotel chains, banks, and credit card companies.

Louise Woerner's HomeCare has won international attention for providing health care services to the elderly

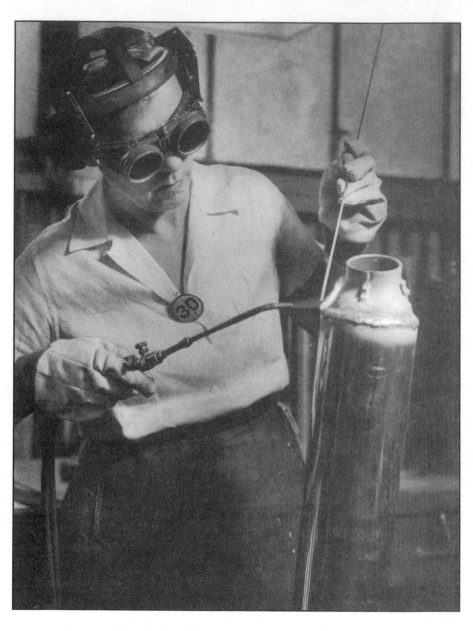

During World War II, a record number of women entered the U.S. work force, often holding down factory jobs that had been held by men who had gone to war. In 1945, women accounted for 36 percent of the nation's employees (compared to 24 percent when the war began).

and people with disabilities, and the company designs health care materials for the federal government. Marilyn Hamilton's California-based company, Motion Designs, has won national acclaim for manufacturing wheelchairs that are more mobile and comfortable. Ella Musolino-Alber, president and co-founder of Sports Etcetera in New York City, organizes and promotes the multi-million dollar Women's Tennis Association Tour Championships each year, as well as many other entertainment events.

These entrepreneurs have shown beyond a doubt that they possess the talent and the skills necessary for making their businesses successful. They have also demonstrated that women have the creativity, strength, and determination to run thriving businesses.

*Mary Kay Ash, now one of the most successful
entrepreneurs in the United States, turned her
"dream company" into a reality.*

1

Mary Kay Ash
Cosmetics Queen

*H*er last name is Ash, but millions of people know her simply as Mary Kay. Her company, Mary Kay Cosmetics, now sells more than $1.7 billion worth of skin-care products each year and has become one of the most successful businesses in the United States founded by a woman. Today, more than 375,000 beauty consultants sell Mary Kay products in 24 countries around the world, and more than 80 of them have become millionaires.

Success did not come easily for Mary Kay, who had many responsibilities while growing up in Houston,

Texas, during the 1920s. When she was seven years old, her father became very ill with tuberculosis and could no longer work, so her mother became the family's sole breadwinner. Because her mother worked 14 hours a day in her job as a restaurant manager, young Mary Kay had to take on much of the responsibility of running the household.

After school each day, Mary Kay would clean the house, care for her sick father, and make dinner. She would call her mother at work for instructions if she didn't know how to prepare a certain dish. Whenever she felt uncertain or overwhelmed, her mother would say, "You can do it!" These reassuring words inspired Mary Kay so much that "You can do it!" would later become a motto of Mary Kay Cosmetics.

When Mary Kay was growing up, her mother would tell her again and again, "Anything anyone else can do, you can do better!" When she was a Girl Scout, her mother urged her to sell more cookies than she had in the previous year and produce more sales than anyone else. Although her mother encouraged her to develop a competitive spirit, she also taught Mary Kay that no one wins all the time and that she must also learn to accept defeat with dignity.

During junior high school, Mary Kay excelled at debate, public speaking, and typing—all skills that would prove to be invaluable to her. She impressed her teachers with her ability to organize her thoughts and present her

*Today, more than 3 million girls throughout the
United States are learning valuable business skills as
members of the Girl Scouts, which was founded
in 1912.*

opinions persuasively, and earned a trophy for being the best typist in her class. In high school, Mary Kay received straight A's and graduated in three years instead of four. Although she dreamed of becoming a doctor, her family could not afford to send her to college.

At age 17, Mary Kay married a member of a local musical group. Soon afterward, the couple moved to Dallas, where their three children were born. By the time her husband entered the military in the early 1940s during World War II, Mary Kay was earning a living by selling household items for Stanley Home Products. One of the benefits of the job was that the hours were flexible, giving her more time to spend with her children.

Mary Kay soon discovered she had a flair for selling. She not only made a good income, but she also persuaded other women to work at Stanley Home Products. Because of her sales success, and her ability to recruit other women to join the company, the business honored her with the title of "Queen of Sales."

During the mid-1940s, Mary Kay began to take college business courses in the morning while continuing to sell in the afternoons. Some of her professors, however, did not like having a mother of three in their classes because they felt she was taking enrollment space away from young men. (At that time, only men were assumed to be family wage earners.) Faced with this type of discrimination, Mary Kay quit telling her instructors and

An early publicity photograph for Stanley Home Products, where Mary Kay Ash developed her sales skills.

classmates about her family. (Around this time, Mary Kay and her husband divorced.)

By 1963, after working for more than 25 years in direct selling, Mary Kay became discouraged because of the lack of advancement opportunity for women. In fact, a younger man she had trained to be her assistant was later promoted to be her boss—at twice her salary. Devastated, Mary Kay "retired."

After leaving her job, Mary Kay decided to write a book for women about the difficulties of achieving success in the business world. As she began making a list of all the good things that had happened in her own career, she started to dream about the ideal company—a company that would reward women for their hard work. Wouldn't it be wonderful, she thought, if someone actually started such a company. Then the billion-dollar idea came! Instead of writing a book describing her "dream company," she would start the company herself.

In the 1960s, most U.S. companies were run by men, and men held almost all of the managerial positions. During her quarter century in direct sales, Mary Kay had worked with numerous capable women whom she felt had been held back from promotions only because they were women. When women complained about the inequities in pay, employers would claim that men needed larger salaries because they had families to support. This reasoning infuriated Mary Kay, who had been the sole provider for her family for many years.

While planning her "dream company," Mary Kay remembered the many male employers she had known who treated women as if they had only half a brain. Though she was a member of her company's board, her male peers often scolded her by saying, "Mary Kay, you're thinking just like a woman." She wanted her company to be a place where such thinking wasn't a liability, and where women with the right skills and determination would not be held back.

When Mary Kay began searching for a product that her new company could sell, she thought of a line of skin-care products she had tried. She noticed that her friends who had used these cosmetics all looked younger than they really were. In fact, when Mary Kay's mother—who had used the products for years—was in her eighties, people said she still looked like a woman of 60. Mary Kay became so enthusiastic about these creams and lotions that she contacted the owner of the formulas and arranged to buy them so she could sell the products in her new business.

Mary Kay invested her entire life savings—$5,000— in her company, and Mary Kay Cosmetics opened for business in 1963 on September 13th (a Friday) in a small store in Dallas. The company started out with nine sales-people, women who were friends of Mary Kay. Mary Kay's 20-year-old son, Richard Rogers, became her financial administrator. (Her two other children, Ben and Marylyn, would also later work for the company.) Although Mary Kay's accountant and lawyer both predicted that her business would fail, the company sold $198,000 worth of products in its first year.

From the start, Mary Kay had a strong understanding about the kind of person she wanted to recruit. She insisted that her salespeople must love what they did because she believed that enjoying your work is an

Even though many people said she would fail, Mary Kay wasn't afraid to do things her way when starting her own business.

important key to success. Mary Kay also knew her customers. She knew, first of all, that they wanted to learn about skin care and cosmetics in a comfortable setting where they would not feel embarrassed or intimidated. So, rather than sell her products in department stores, she chose to hold cosmetics demonstrations—initially called "beauty shows"—in the privacy of women's homes.

Second, Mary Kay decided that each beauty show would be for only five or six prospective customers. This arrangement was very different from the approach used by Stanley Home Products and other in-home selling companies, which presented their products to groups of 25 to

30 women. She knew that most women did not own enough coffee cups to serve so many people at once, and she also realized that most women would not want to talk about things as personal as skin care and makeup in such a large gathering.

As Mary Kay Ash's name became better known in the Dallas area, several department stores asked her to present her line of cosmetics at their stores. She turned down all of these requests because she believed that since women put on their makeup at home, the home is the proper place for women to purchase cosmetics and learn how to apply makeup.

Mary Kay's third idea was calling her sales force beauty consultants instead of salespeople. She wanted her consultants to be helpful to their customers—not merely to sell products—and to become skin care *experts*, whose opinions their customers would trust. Her beauty consultants would evaluate the skin needs of each potential customer and try their best to answer any questions their customers had. Then they would show the women how to cleanse their skin properly, and apply makeup to enhance their appearance. Mary Kay believed that if her consultants instructed their customers correctly, her products would sell themselves. (Today, the company's training manual is more than 200 pages long and Mary Kay is the best-selling brand of facial skin care and color cosmetics in the U.S., based on the most recent available industry data and actual Mary Kay sales.)

To provide the best service, Mary Kay also knew that her products must be readily available to prospective customers. She knew that people wanted their cosmetics immediately upon purchase—not three weeks after they had paid for them. Therefore, she asked early consultants always to carry a line of about 10 different items with them.

Each Mary Kay beauty consultant is essentially an independent business person and her own boss, setting her own hours. The consultants have no designated territories to limit the areas where they can sell their products. Instead, they are free to sell their products anywhere. (Mary Kay products were initially made by a private manufacturing firm, but the company soon began to manufacture its own products. Today, Mary Kay's state-of-the-art manufacturing plant is one of the largest in the southwestern United States.)

Consultants buy their cosmetics directly from Mary Kay Cosmetics and pay for them immediately. Then they make "house calls" to sell customers the products they have just purchased. Because customers are required to pay for the product at the time of purchase, Mary Kay consultants do not have to bill them or worry about getting paid several weeks or even months after making a sale. By not extending credit, they can earn more money. Mary Kay's success proves that her innovative ideas have worked.

In 1964, about a year after the company began, all 200 members of the Mary Kay team at that time gathered for the company's first convention. In her welcoming speech, Mary Kay predicted that by the end of 1965, there would be 3,000 people working for the company. But she was mistaken—by then, Mary Kay Cosmetics had grown to number 11,000 people! Mary Kay says she can always spot new consultants at the conventions because they simply sit in their seats and listen. But by the end of a meeting, both newcomers and experienced consultants are singing and clapping their hands.

For Mary Kay Ash, here with her son Richard Rogers, the Golden Rule of life's priorities puts God first, family second, and career third.

More than 40,000 consultants for Mary Kay Cosmetics attend the company's annual seminar in Dallas each year.

In addition to the yearly seminars, Mary Kay Cosmetics also organized Monday meetings for her consultants. The basic ingredient at each sales meeting is enthusiasm. Mary Kay tells her consultants, "If you had a bad week, you need the sales meeting. If you had a good week, the sales meeting needs you." She urges her consultants to wear "happy faces," even when it is not easy to do. Therefore, the Monday meetings begin with what Mary Kay calls a "crow period." This is a time for the consultants to share their sales successes of the past week. As soon as one person finishes, another tells about something great that happened to her during the previous week. Mary Kay knew that even if one consultant had a bad week, after hearing other consultants "crow," she will think, "If she can do it, I can do it, too." In the world of Mary Kay, a happy face and a happy attitude inspire others. When a Mary Kay consultant leaves one of these Monday meetings, she has the whole week to let the excitement work for her.

Mary Kay believes that people feel better about themselves and their careers when they receive rewards in addition to money. Because of this, she has developed contests in which employees and consultants compete against one another in creative ways, such as trying to write the best company song. Mary Kay has also created extra incentives that give all of her consultants a chance to be winners. For example, successful beauty consultants can win prizes such as jewelry and vacations, as well as computers and fax machines.

Mary Kay's top performers are rewarded with a diamond pin in the shape of a bumblebee, a creature whose very ability to fly has caused some people to wonder. As Mary Kay writes in her autobiography:

> Within our organization, the bumblebee has become the ultimate symbol of accomplishment. We selected it because of what the bumblebee represents for all women. You see, years ago, aerodynamic engineers studied this creature and decided that it simply *should not be able* to fly! Its wings are too weak and its body too heavy for flight. Everything seems to tell the bumblebee, "You'll never get off the ground." But I like to think that maybe—just maybe—our Divine Creator whispered, "You can do it!"; so it did!

Another special reward treasured by Mary Kay consultants is a pink Cadillac. Mary Kay, who used to drive a black car, often grew frustrated when other drivers would cut in front of her at intersections, almost as if they didn't see her. One morning when this happened, Mary Kay drove straight to her Cadillac dealer. She told the dealer she wanted a *pink* Cadillac—the color of the company's lip and eye palette. "Mary Kay," said the dealer, "you don't want to do this! Let me tell you how much it's going to cost to repaint it when it arrives and what if you don't like it?" But Mary Kay was determined and, of course, her pink Cadillac was a huge success. Drivers didn't cut in front of her anymore, and the sales force all wanted to know how they could receive one. The following year, this very special car became a prize for her top sales people. Today, more than 7,500 successful Mary Kay consultants drive these pink Cadillacs and Grand Prixs and red Grand Ams worth more than $116 million. And at General Motors, the Detroit auto maker that creates them, the color is officially called "Mary Kay pink."

Today, Mary Kay remains active, serving as Mary Kay Cosmetics' chairman emeritus. She continues to keep office hours and serves as primary motivator for the sales force. She also oversees a large support staff, which sends personal responses to more than 7,000 letters Mary Kay receives monthly.

During the 1980s, Mary Kay finally finished the book that she had begun thinking about during the early

1960s. *Mary Kay on People Management* was published in 1984 and has sold more than one million copies. Today, *Fortune* magazine lists Mary Kay Cosmetics, which now has more than $1.7 billion in annual sales, as one of the most admired corporations in the United States. Harvard University's business school has described Mary Kay as one of the best business leaders in the United States. And the company has twice been listed in *The 100 Best Companies to Work For in America.*

Early in the company's development, when it had become obvious that Mary Kay's venture was succeeding, business experts would ask her questions like, "What was your sales goal the first year?" And May Kay would always answer that a dollar figure was never what she had in mind. "What I tried to do," she said firmly, "was give women an unlimited opportunity to succeed."

Although art collectors had once wanted only porcelain originating from Europe, Helen Boehm has won international acclaim for the porcelain figures her company designs in the United States.

2

Helen Boehm
Sculpting Success

*W*hen Bill Clinton was inaugurated president of the United States in 1993, he was presented with a porcelain sculpture named "New Generation Eagle." The piece was designed by the Boehm Studio, one of the most famous porcelain companies in the world. The Boehm company has been creating beautiful porcelain pieces of art for nearly 45 years.

Helen Boehm, who started the company with her husband in Trenton, New Jersey, in 1950, still owns and operates this specialized business. The porcelain

Helen Boehm presents a porcelain bear to U.S. general Norman Schwarzkopf (top) and the "Patriot Eagle" to General Colin Powell.

sculptures her company creates are on display in more than 130 museums and famous sites all over the world, including the White House in Washington, D.C., Buckingham Palace in London, the Élysée Palace in Paris, the Vatican Museum in Rome, and the Great Hall in Beijing, China.

Elena Franzolin (who would later change her name to Helen) was born in Brooklyn, New York, to a family of Italian immigrants who had come to the United States in 1909. Her father, Pietro, was a cabinetmaker, but he made so little money that the family was always struggling. When Helen was 13, her family's financial situation became even worse after her father died. Her mother, Francesca, could not earn very much money, so Helen and her five older siblings had to find part-time jobs to help pay for the family's expenses. At an early age, Helen had learned to sew. After winning a junior-high dress design competition, she decided to earn extra money after school by sewing clothing for her friends, charging them 50 cents a dress.

When Helen graduated from high school, she realized she would need to earn more money than what she could make by sewing. She found a job working as a receptionist for Nathan Gillis, her family's eye doctor. While growing up, she had enjoyed going to this optometrist, and she used to pretend to give eye exams to her dolls. Helen also attended the Mechanical School of Optics in Brooklyn Heights, where she studied eyewear fashion and learned to make lenses for eyeglasses. After graduating, she became one of the first women in New York to receive an optician's license. (An optician makes the lenses prescribed by an optometrist.)

When she was 22, Helen met a 31-year-old veterinary assistant named Edward Boehm who worked at a farm that bred animals. In addition to his veterinary skills, Boehm was also a talented artist who had taught himself how to make realistic clay sculptures of animals.

The couple was married on October 29, 1944. Soon afterward, Helen was hired as an optician at the prestigious Meyrowitz Optical Center in New York City. There she spent much of her time designing glasses frames in the company's laboratory. One of her most memorable experiences as an optician was helping film star Clark Gable find a suitable pair of sunglasses.

Edward's career, however, took a turn for the worse during the late 1940s when a fire on the farm where he was working destroyed his 15 years of notes about animal breeding. By this time, the Boehms' apartment was filled with Edward's sculptures of birds, dogs, cows, horses, and other animals, and Helen was confident that her husband could start a new career and earn a living by selling his sculptures. Rather than using clay, Edward decided to make his sculptures out of hard-paste porcelain because porcelain figures would look more realistic.

Working in porcelain follows a complicated and ancient art form. As early as A.D. 600, artists in China had used porcelain—a combination of clay, feldspar, and other substances—to make sculptures. Because porcelain sculpture is done almost entirely by hand, an individual design can take weeks to complete. Then the porcelain is painted, which is another step that requires a great deal of precision. Finally, the sculpture is baked in a kind of furnace, called a kiln, at an extremely high temperature (2400 degrees Fahrenheit).

Because they had no money, no customers, and nothing to sell, the Boehms knew that getting a bank loan to start their business would be difficult. They had no way of proving they had the necessary skills to run such a business, but they did have three assets: Ed Boehm's enormous artistic ability, Helen Boehm's sales and marketing experience, and their combined desire to succeed. Their first loan, which came in late 1949, was $500 from a veterinarian colleague of Edward. Shortly afterward, Helen convinced a local bank to lend them $1,000, which was enough money to get their company started.

In 1950, the Boehms opened their business in a small, one-room studio in Trenton, New Jersey, a city that had been the center of ceramic artwork production in the United States since the mid-1800s. They originally named the company Osso China Company—*osso* is the Italian word for bone—but changed it to Edward Marshall Boehm, Inc. two years later.

The new company faced a major disadvantage, however, because U.S. porcelain collectors were used to purchasing sculptures from Europe or Asia instead of in the United States. For decades, Spode, Wedgwood, Worcester, and other famous companies overseas had been manufacturing intricate porcelain figures. These companies employed most of the world's top porcelain sculptors, and they knew how to sell their products.

In order to succeed, Helen and Edward Boehm knew they would have to produce and begin selling their porcelain sculptures before they ran out of money. To compete with the well-known names in the industry, they also realized their products would have to be truly unique and of exceptional quality. They quickly had to earn a reputation among experienced collectors, museum curators, and public figures, who would spread the word about their porcelain pieces.

During her lunch hours, Helen would leave her office and introduce herself to prospective clients for the Boehm's new company. In January 1951, the couple had their first real break when Vincent Andrus, the curator for the American collection at the Metropolitan Museum of Art in New York, bought two of Edward's first sculptures, "Percheron Stallion" and "Hereford Bull." Although each sculpture sold for only $30, the prestige of having Edward's work shown in one of the world's most famous museums could not be measured in dollars.

On January 21, 1951, the *New York Times* carried an article about the Metropolitan's new acquisitions. In the story, curator Andrus said, "The realistic ceramics are equal to the finest of superior English work." When curators at other museums read about the porcelain figures, the Boehm name started to become known by art collectors throughout the world. Soon afterward, the

Edward Marshall Boehm would study live animals in order to depict them accurately in his sculptures.

Boehm studio began to sell porcelain pieces to museums in many countries. After almost ten years at Meyrowitz, Helen quit her job as an optician to devote more time to the growing business.

By 1953, the Boehm studio was doing so well that the Boehms were able to move out of their apartment and purchase their first home. It was at this time that Helen wrote a letter to President Dwight Eisenhower, suggesting he commission them to make porcelain sculptures for visiting foreign officials. The president liked this idea, and, in 1957, he asked Edward to do a sculpture of Prince Philip, the husband of England's Queen Elizabeth II. Because Prince Philip's love of polo was well known, Edward sculpted the prince on a polo pony. President Eisenhower presented the sculpture, "Polo Player," to Queen Elizabeth and her husband when they visited the United States that year.

Years later, Helen learned that Queen Elizabeth was somewhat disappointed because the helmet on the sculpture was white, and the prince *always* wore a blue helmet when he played polo. Helen pleased the queen when she offered to have the helmet repainted.

In 1959, Catholic monsignor Emilio Cardelia of Trenton ordered several Boehm pieces to present to Pope John XXIII for display in the Vatican Museum's art collection. When the pope saw one of the sculptures, "Cerulean Warblers with Wild Roses," he said, "One

*Boehm holds Her Majesty the Queen's Cup, one of
many cups won by the Boehm Palm Beach Polo Team
and the Boehm Polo Team of England during the
1982 season. Two porcelain polo players appear in the
lower right.*

hesitates to go too close for fear the birds might fly
away."

During the 1960s, more and more art collectors
bought Boehm pieces, and the Boehms were thrilled by
their international success. Helen traveled around the
world, selling their products and bringing back ideas,
and Edward created the designs and directed the

production work. For almost 20 years, Edward and Helen were an unbeatable team, and their sculptures began to sell for as much as $1,000 each.

Everything changed in 1969, however, when Edward died of a heart attack at the age of 55. Many people working in the porcelain industry thought the Boehm studio could not continue without Edward and his world-renowned talent. After all, Edward had become famous as the first American to create porcelain figures that art experts considered to be as well designed as the works of the European masters. His sculptures of animals were so realistic that many people said they looked as though a taxidermist had made them from real animals.

After her husband's death, Helen Boehm carried the business forward with the help of a skilled staff of dedicated artists. Maurice Eyeington, a sculptor who had assisted Edward Boehm, became the company's head sculptor, and he would often accompany Boehm on her business trips around the globe.

Because of the high demand for porcelain in Europe, Boehm decided to start a Boehm studio in the town of Malvern, England, in 1970. Many famous artists lived and worked in this area, where the creation of porcelain art was a centuries-old tradition. Within a few years, the Boehm studio in England was almost as well known as the one in the United States. At the English studio, artisans created special gifts for members of the

Helen Boehm displays a porcelain panda bear. Many art collectors are impressed by the the intricate details in Boehm sculptures.

English royal family. While visiting the Boehm studio in 1979, Prince Charles saw a Boehm flower and said in admiration, "Only the fragrance is missing."

But now Helen faced another crisis. One night, she felt a painful sensation in one of her eyes, and her vision was fuzzy. Because of her training as an optician, she immediately recognized she was experiencing the early signs of a detached retina, a condition that causes clouding in the center of the eye and reduces one's vision. She knew she needed immediate eye surgery to treat the problem. Fortunately, the operation was a success, and Helen's vision was much improved.

All through the 1970s, the Boehm business continued to grow. Helen hired assistants to help her. She enlarged the studios in Trenton and patterned the newer studio in Malvern after the original. She insisted that quality never be sacrificed, even though creating pieces at a faster rate would have given them more items to sell. As a result of her high standards, heads of governments and art collectors worldwide continued to order Boehm work. When President Richard Nixon made his historic trip to China in 1972, he presented Chairman Mao Tsetung with a pair of Boehm porcelain swans called "Mute Swans, Birds of Peace." The Chinese, who had been producing porcelain for hundreds of years, had a deep appreciation of this art form. Chairman Mao thought the swans looked real enough to have once been alive. This was praise indeed for the Edward Marshall Boehm studios, and Helen Boehm would later become one of the first businesswomen invited to China.

Another great moment for the Boehm studio came during the mid-1970s, when the Egyptian government asked Helen Boehm to reproduce in porcelain 38 of the treasures of the pharaoh Tutankhamen (now better known as "King Tut") so art collectors could own or display these pieces of ancient Egyptian art. Boehm was initially hesitant to recreate the artifacts because her company had created sculptures only of animals and plants. She decided to accept the offer, however, and was pleased with the results.

Boehm traveled to Saudi Arabia during the late 1970s to open up a new market, despite the advice of her business colleagues. Saudi business officials seldom agree to do business with women, but Boehm successfully began selling her porcelain figures to art buyers there.

During the 1980s, U.S. president Ronald Reagan and First Lady Nancy Reagan became two of Boehm's biggest fans. The company received national attention in 1987 when one their most famous sculptures, "Mute Swans" (identical to the one given to Chairman Mao a decade earlier), was accidentally damaged when it was shipped back to the United States after being on display in the Soviet Union.

The Boehm Studio has remained successful in the 1990s. Nearly 100 artisans now work in the Boehm studios in the United States and England. In some cases,

At a six-week Boehm exhibition in the Soviet Union, Helen Boehm shows her 1985 autobiography, With a Little Luck: An American Odyssey, *to Raisa Gorbachev, wife of Soviet leader Mikhail Gorbachev.*

they will make no more than 1,000 sculptures from one design, and the most costly may be limited to only 25 pieces. These may sell for up to $125,000 each, and some sculptures have been auctioned off for as much as $150,000.

Helen Boehm has said entrepreneurs must produce products they believe in and must work "day in, day out, many hours each day." She explains that running a business is "not a matter of starting at nine in the morning and quitting at five in the afternoon." Instead, work must be at the center of an entrepreneur's life.

About her career, Helen once said, "The Boehm reputation is now assured, but it was earned." She added that "life is a collection of risks. I am not afraid to take them. If you lose, you must work to win again." For, she concluded, "Being an entrepreneur is at once two things: the most satisfying and most exhausting activity there is in life."

Helen Boehm hands a porcelain rose to actress Sophia Loren, one of many celebrities who have become fans of Boehm's work.

Years after moving to the United States, Leeann Chin realized there was a market for food prepared the way it is in her native China.

3

Leeann Chin
Beyond Chow Mein

*E*arly in 1978, Leeann Chin received a telephone call in her Minneapolis home from a man who was vacationing in Palm Springs, California. The caller was Carl Pohlad, a successful banker and the owner of the Minnesota Twins baseball team. Pohlad was planning to throw a party for some of his friends, and he wanted Chin to fly to Palm Springs to cater the event. His guests, he said, would include several famous actors, including Robert Redford and Michael Caine.

Over the years, Leeann Chin has grown accustomed to requests for her special Chinese dinners, but this was the most dramatic. "I could have made a lot of money," she said later, "but it also would have taken me away from my basic business, which needs me on hand. It was hard to do, but I turned Mr. Pohlad down." Flying to Palm Springs would have taken Leeann from her previous commitments at home and, as a businesswoman, she knows how important it is to keep one's commitments.

In the Twin Cities area of Minneapolis and St. Paul, Minnesota, the name Leeann Chin has come to stand for fine Chinese food. Since opening her first restaurant in 1980, the president of Leeann Chin, Inc. has become one of the most popular and successful entrepreneurs in the Midwest.

Leeann Chin was born Lee Wai-Hing in Canton, China, on February 13, 1933. (*Lee* was her surname and *Wai-Hing* was her first name.) When she was 11, she began working in her father's retail and wholesale markets, and there began to develop the culinary skills that would one day make her a great chef.

At age 18, Wai-Hing moved briefly to Hong Kong and fell in love with a man named Tony Chin, whom she would marry. In 1956, the couple and their first child fled Communist China and emigrated to the United States. They moved to Minneapolis, where Tony's sister lived. Tony got a job in his sister's restaurant, and Wai-Hing "Americanized" her first name to Leeann. She got her first job in the United States working in the alterations department of a clothing store, after having studied both English and tailoring at a local vocational school. She later put her new sewing skills to work by beginning a dressmaking business in her home. As the business grew, it eventually provided money to send their five children to college.

In the early 1970s, Chin began to create special lunches for the many customers for whom she was sewing and altering clothes. Her customers were so delighted with her Chinese delicacies such as shrimp toast, egg drop soup, and lemon chicken that they urged her to teach cooking classes. The more she thought about this suggestion, the more sense it made.

Chin began to teach the art of Chinese cooking in the homes of her friends and customers in late 1972. Her classes were so successful that she soon began teaching evening classes in Chinese cooking at a local high school and at a community education center. Soon afterward, she quit her seamstress work and became a professional caterer. As she went into people's homes and private clubs to prepare and serve meals for special occasions, she became even better known in an area of the country where few people knew how to prepare authentic Chinese food.

By the late 1970s, Chin was catering large parties, banquets, and receptions. In addition to the word-of-mouth advertising by her many customers and friends, she

Although Leeann Chin left her home-land of China (shown here in the 1940s), Chinese customs and traditions have remained very important to her.

also received positive publicity in area newspapers and was asked to appear on local television programs. The only person who did not approve of her business was her husband, who felt the proper place for a Chinese wife was in the home.

In 1979, after teaching Chinese cooking to nearly 4,000 people, Chin decided to quit her classes and open her own restaurant, which would serve Cantonese and Sichuan dishes buffet-style for lunch and dinner. Although she was already a successful caterer, her husband did not think she had enough training to run her own business and predicted she would surely fail. Despite her husband's disapproval, Leeann Chin decided to go ahead with her plan. "People said I couldn't do it, so I wanted to prove them wrong," she later said. She received a $165,000 government loan from the Small Business Administration and convinced several investors, including Carl Pohlad and Sean Connery, to help finance her new business.

The location that Chin chose for her first restaurant was an upscale shopping mall in Minnetonka, a Minneapolis suburb. A local architect named David Shea designed a space that could seat 80 diners. Chin decorated the restaurant with her collection of beautiful

After spending several years teaching others how to prepare Chinese cuisine, Leeann Chin decided to start catering events herself.

Chinese artifacts made from ivory, jade, and porcelain. Leeann Chin Chinese Cuisine opened for business in 1980 and had sales of more than $1.5 million during its first year of operation.

Through her teaching, Leeann developed many recipes, and she began to think of how she could put these to work in some way to help her business continue to grow. It happens that General Mills, one of the largest food companies in the world, is also headquartered in a Minneapolis suburb. Several General Mills executives had become aware of Leeann's talents because their spouses had taken her cooking classes. So Leeann approached General Mills with her recipes and together they created a new cookbook, to be called *Betty Crocker's Chinese Cookbook, Recipes by Leeann Chin*. (Betty Crocker is a fictional woman pictured on many General Mills products.) Chin's cookbook was published in 1981 and has sold more than 350,000 copies worldwide. The cookbook helped to promote Chin's restaurant, which had just opened the previous year.

In 1983, Chin's business was growing so rapidly that she decided to invest $300,000 to expand her restaurant to nearly double its seating capacity. The following year, Chin opened another restaurant in a historic, recently restored railroad station in downtown St. Paul.

Since carry-out food accounted for nearly 20 percent of the business in her Minnetonka restaurant, Chin recognized there was a demand for this type of service. In

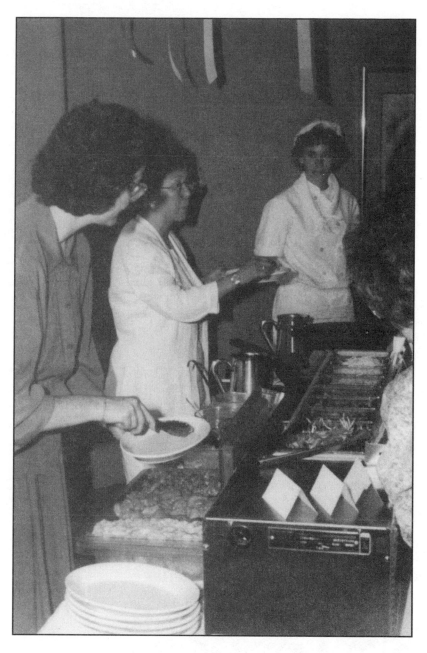

Leeann Chin, an experienced teacher, gives cooking instructions to her staff.

1984, she arranged to lease space in Dayton's (a famous department store in downtown Minneapolis), where she opened the first Leeann Chin Carryout Chinese Cuisine, offering gourmet Chinese food to go. The business quickly caught on, and soon was averaging more than 500 customers each day.

In late 1984, Leeann, who had been studying the long-range opportunities for her business, felt it was time to expand and open several new restaurants. But this would be extremely expensive, and she had neither the

With more than 100 recipes, Leeann Chin's first cookbook has become a popular item for both experienced and beginning chefs.

large amount of money this would require, nor the overall business experience to do it all herself. So in 1985, she and General Mills got together again, and this time, instead of just doing a new cookbook, they offered to buy her company.

Because Minnesotans were so pleased with Chin's restaurants and the Betty Crocker cookbook had sold so well, General Mills executives hoped to turn Leeann Chin's Chinese Cuisine into a national restaurant chain. Chin was excited by the offer because she thought a large company like General Mills would be able help her company grow. Leeann accepted their offer for her business. Her 300 employees became employees of General Mills, and she was hired as an executive for the corporation. Immediately after the acquisition, General Mills opened a third Leeann Chin Chinese Cuisine in the International Centre in downtown Minneapolis.

However, as often happens when a large company buys a very small one, things did not work out as General Mills had planned. And in 1988, three years after the purchase, it had become clear to the company's management that the business did not fit their corporate objectives. So, General Mills sold the business Leeann had originally started back to her.

During the period that General Mills was operating her business, Leeann realized that she was learning a lot by working with their executives and managers. And she saw as the months went by that the partnership between

Leeann Chin stands at the reception desk of her restaurant in the International Centre of Minneapolis.

Leeann Chin autographs a copy of her second book,
Betty Crocker's New Chinese Cookbook,
Recipes by Leeann Chin.

her and the huge company was probably not in the best
interest of either of them. So the buy-back was good for
both, and Leeann still maintains very positive relations
with General Mills. In fact, the company asked her to
write a second cookbook, *Betty Crocker's New Chinese
Cookbook, Recipes by Leeann Chin*, which was published in
1990.

With Leeann in charge once more, and armed with
the knowledge she had gained in working with General

Mills, her business—now called Leeann Chin, Inc.—began to grow. She entered into an agreement with Byerly's, a large Minnesota supermarket chain, to sell her takeout food. Leeann says today that after buying back her company she really began to enjoy the business again. "It was so good to get back into action again and have the opportunity to work with my staff of fine people."

By the end of 1994, Leeann Chin, Inc. had 3 restaurants in the Twin Cities, along with 19 carry-out locations (including 10 at Byerly's stores). She also had opened 6 carry-out locations in the QFC grocery stores of Seattle. Her company had more than 700 employees and did more than $25 million in business yearly. One of her top employees is her daughter, Laura, an executive vice-president of the company.

In July 1995, Leeann launched a new, moderately priced restaurant called Asia Grille, which combines Chinese, Vietnamese, Korean, Thai, and Japanese food. She hopes that the blended-menu concept, begun in the Minneapolis suburb of Eden Prairie, will be successful enough for her to expand Asia Grille to other locations.

It is, of course, an understatement to say merely that Leeann Chin has achieved great success. Her accomplishments are truly remarkable. She serves on the boards of directors for several Minnesota non-profit organizations. She has also been named to the Minnesota Business Hall of Fame. In 1993, Leeann was chosen as one of

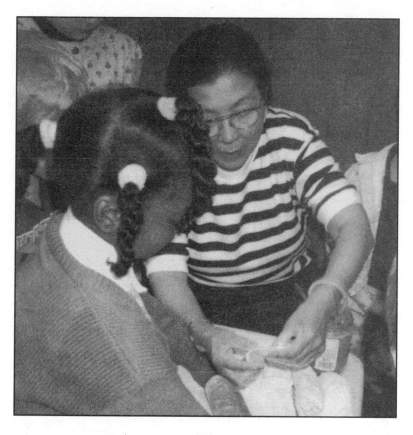

Leeann Chin makes dumplings as part of a "Gateway to China" exhibit at the Minnesota Children's Museum in 1993.

Minnesota's ten best entrepreneurs in a national awards program sponsored by a major law firm and large accounting firm, along with *Inc.* magazine. Perhaps the honor that most pleases Leeann is that of Woman Business Owner of the Year, presented to her in 1988 by the National Association of Women Business Owners (NAWBO).

Leeann Chin and her daughter, Laura (left), celebrate at the company's anniversary party. Leeann has asked Laura to take over the company when she retires.

Along with being an accomplished businesswoman, Chin is involved with such diverse organizations and programs as the YMCA, public television, and DARE, a national drug-abuse education program. As a member of the Committee of 100, a national group giving voice to the Chinese-American population, Chin traveled to China in the spring of 1994 to promote better relations between the United States and China.

Like many business owners, Chin has written a *mission statement* to explain the philosophy behind her business. Her statement says, in part:

> Our customers will receive consistently high quality food and service, bringing continued customer loyalty. Our employees will work in a creative, challenging environment, while receiving ongoing opportunities for personal and professional growth. . . . Our commitment to excellence will result in growth and prosperity, enhancing our position of leadership in the ever-changing food service industry.

Today, reflecting on the past, Leeann says that her biggest mistake in business was selling her company, because it left her with little to do and no professional and personal challenges. Carrying out her own ideas had always been a source of great satisfaction. For young people, she offers sound advice: "Discipline yourself, work hard. Don't remember what you've done for others; only remember what others have done for you."

After losing her home and facing an enormous debt, Ellen Terry created a multi-million dollar company selling real estate.

4

Ellen Terry
From Ruin to Real Estate Riches

One afternoon in late 1974, a young wife and mother was entertaining members of the Junior League women's civic group at her home in the Highland Park neighborhood of Dallas, Texas. When Ellen Terry heard a knock on her front door and opened it, she faced a man dressed in overalls who demanded the keys to her Mercedes. He said that because no payments had been made on the car loan for several months, he had been sent to repossess the car. In shock, Ellen looked out in front of her house and saw a tow truck haul off her Mercedes.

Ellen soon discovered that she and her husband, a former bank president, were in deep financial trouble and owed the Internal Revenue Service more than $100,000 in back federal income taxes. They were forced to sell their $200,000 home, and along with their two small children they moved into a rental house. During her marriage, Ellen had grown accustomed to expensive clothes, weekly tennis lessons, and other luxuries of life, but now all of that had to change.

By 1976, Ellen and her husband had separated. She moved into an efficiency apartment and sent her two children, ages six and eight, to live with their grandparents, where they would stay for seven months. Ellen found herself with no job and felt she had no future. Years later, Ellen said that this crisis was probably the best thing that had ever happened to her:

> I was taught to be a fighter, not a quitter. My dad was only five feet five, and he wore size five cowboy boots. He told me the only inches that matter are the six inches between your two ears. He said you could look at things positively or negatively. He taught me that you can look at a glass of water and consider it half full or half empty— it's up to you. This was the beginning of me getting in touch with who I really was. I wasn't put on earth, as no one is, to be taken care of.

Ellen had been born and raised in Paris, Texas, and she moved to Dallas to attend Southern Methodist

When Ellen Terry was a teenager in the 1950s, few young women even dreamed they might become successful in the world of business.

University. Although she had been a gym teacher after graduating from college, she had no business skills and little work experience. Still, she faced up to her difficult financial situation and accepted it as the biggest challenge of her life.

Needing a job immediately, Ellen went to work in a travel agency at $1,000 a month. But the salary was not enough to comfortably support Ellen and her growing children. She wanted them to be able to live in a nice home, go to summer camp, have braces on their teeth if they needed them, and eventually attend a good college.

Instead of a salary, Ellen needed a job that would pay her based on how hard she worked and how productive she was. A job in the sales industry would give her a commission—a percentage of the sales she made—and would not put a ceiling on the amount of income she could earn. If she wanted a job that would pay her more money, she would have to be willing to work longer hours.

Ellen thought long and hard about the kind of job she could find, and someone suggested that she might enjoy real estate. Because Ellen was interested in houses and also liked working with people, the real-estate business seemed to be a perfect match.

Ellen applied for a job with Coldwell Banker, a national real-estate agency that had recently opened an office in Dallas. After several interviews, the company decided Ellen was qualified for the job. When she was offered the position, her supervisors warned her that the real-estate business was very difficult and newcomers often needed several months to make their first sale. Because of this, the company would give her a "draw" for six months. That meant a small portion of the commissions she would earn when she sold a house would be paid to her in advance. Her $500-a-month draw was only half as much as she had been making at the travel agency.

It did not take Ellen Terry six months to make her first sale, however. In just 30 days, she had sold a house for $400,000. Two weeks later, she sold another for almost $300,000. Her commission for the two sales was more than $12,000, which in one month was about the same amount she would have earned after working a full year for the travel agency.

Ellen spent two years working at Coldwell Banker in Dallas. During that time, she became Coldwell's top salesperson in the state of Texas and the company's second-best salesperson in the United States. It seemed like she was made for real estate, and real estate seemed made for Ellen Terry. With her growing income, she could now afford many of the advantages she had wanted for her children.

In 1979, Ellen left Coldwell Banker to start a small real-estate company with two other colleagues. Although this new venture was successful, she soon realized she wanted to have a business of her own. Two years later, in 1981, Ellen started her own company, Ellen Terry, Realtors.

Opening with five agents, Ellen rented 500 square feet of office space and worked hard to make her company a success. Just three months later, the company needed far more space because 23 new associates had joined the firm. Ellen Terry, Realtors had sales of more than $30 million in its first year of business, and the company would continue to grow.

Ellen is the first to admit that some luck was involved with her success. In the early 1980s, the real-estate business was booming throughout the United

States—and especially in Texas. After an economic boom, however, the marketplace typically begins to slow down for a few years, and that is what happened in Texas in 1985. For four years, the real-estate business had been booming in Dallas, one of the oil capitals of the world. Then, with the fall of oil prices worldwide during the mid-1980s, the city's economy began to falter. Anything that hurt the Texas oil business also hurt the economy of Dallas.

With business declining, Ellen decided to follow the advice she had received from her father and mother years ago and tried to focus on the positive instead of the negative. Looking on these setbacks as opportunities, Ellen urged her salespeople to get back to basics by really serving their customers and being even more helpful than usual by going that extra mile. Prospective home buyers, she said, would want more service and information from the agents who were trying to sell them houses, and potential home sellers would also be expecting more help. Ellen encouraged her employees to educate themselves further about the market and to take continuing education courses to broaden their horizons. She also suggested they read inspirational books and become involved in the community.

During this period, Ellen brought in professional speakers to talk to her associates about many subjects, not just real estate. She established these seminars because she wanted her associates to be well informed. She

Ellen Terry and her daughter, Amy, stand in front of the house where Ellen grew up.

*Ellen Terry gives the 1985 commencement speech at
Paris High School in her hometown.*

wanted them to learn how to deal not only with the
problems of selling houses, but also with the larger issues
concerning their personal and family lives.

Ellen's ideas paid off. For several years many of
her sales associates have been honored for their outstanding achievements and named among the city's best
realtors by the Dallas Board of Realtors. As time passed,
Ellen—who considered herself to be a workaholic—

realized that she wanted a more even pace to her life. Over the years, she had become almost "addicted" to the adrenaline rush she experienced from putting in 12 to 14 hours of work each day at her high-pressure job, and she needed a change.

In the early 1980s, Ellen's son became heavily involved with drugs and alcohol. During her son's recovery, Ellen decided to dedicate herself to combating psychological problems and chemical addictions. She now refers to her son's problem as "God's wake-up call" for her to step back and take a look at all aspects of her own life.

In 1986, the company established the Awareness Program, and speakers were brought in to educate her associates and their clients about drug and alcohol abuse, workaholism, eating disorders such as anorexia and bulimia, and other compulsive behaviors. At first, these meetings were just for her own associates and invited guests, but she gradually expanded them to include the general public. These programs grew so popular they eventually were held in a high school auditorium, with as many as 1,000 teenagers and parents attending.

After participating in many workshops about dys-functional families, Ellen hosted Dallas's first Co-Dependency Anonymous (CODA) seminar in 1987. CODA was intended as a "12-step program"—similar to Alcoholics Anonymous—that helps people cope with per-sonal and family problems. More than 100 people came to the first meeting. Since then, several other CODA groups have been formed.

While having balance in her life is important to her, Ellen has continued to be very involved in her business. Since its creation in 1981, Ellen Terry, Realtors has sold more than $1.5 billion worth of properties. Surviving several ups and downs in real estate, Ellen has learned that she cannot control the economy—but she can control what she *does* about it.

During the slow-down in the economy, Ellen created a new division in her company for leasing property. Her idea was to give people the opportunity to live in a house before actually buying it. Then, at some future time, they could decide to purchase the house they had been renting. This division of her real-estate firm has grown while other areas stayed the same. Another new department of the company sells only ranch property. This new division now generates millions of dollars for the company each year.

"What we tried to do all along," Ellen has said, "was to create a very specialized real-estate business." She told her agents to focus not on money, but on service. They needed to be honest professionals whom home buyers could trust. She encouraged her agents to set personal goals for themselves and always to strive for excellence.

Ellen's advice to her associates is working. In 1993, her 50 agents sold more than $200 million worth of real

*An avid golfer in her spare time, Ellen Terry started
the Annual Women's Golf Classic in 1991. The Ellen
Terry Foundation runs the tournament each year and
donates the proceeds to non-profit organizations that
benefit women or children.*

estate, and more than 120 of the houses they sold were multi-million dollar residences. Ellen expects each agent to reach the goal of at least $2 million in annual sales. Her top associates sell from $10 million to $15 million each year.

"I think most successful people are those who have experienced many failures," Ellen has said. "They don't

Every year, Ellen Terry awards a Texas school with a plaque in a student's name and a $500 donation, which goes toward school programs.

let failure get them down—they always keep coming back for one more round, never giving up. If you learn from your failures and keep trying, I like to think of this as *falling forward.*"

Ellen has always been proud that her company is often called the "Neiman Marcus" of the real-estate business in Dallas, after the national department store chain that started in Dallas and is known for its exclusive merchandise and exceptional service. Today, many of her colleagues think Ellen Terry is one of the best realtors in Texas. "Success is never easy," she says. "But if you stay focused and committed, you learn that tough times don't last. Never give up, and always remember the more you reach out and help others, the more success will come back to you!"

Ella Musolino-Alber combines initiative and level-headedness to make her company—and her clients—successful.

5

Ella Musolino-Alber
Contender off the Court

*I*n the spring of 1986, Ella Musolino-Alber faced a crisis. She was in charge of one of the world's most important tennis tournaments at Madison Square Garden in New York City when the unexpected took place. During the second day of the tournament, the city's temperatures soared, and the arena's air-conditioning system suddenly stopped working. Thousands of tennis fans began to wilt from the intense heat, but Ella remained calm under pressure.

Instead of panicking, she asked Bobby Goldwater, who was part of the arena's staff, to walk over to the public-address system and tell the fans to "take off their jackets, roll up their sleeves, and have a good time!" The fans began to relax, and Ella's quick thinking saved the day.

Taking charge and solving problems is routine to Ella. As the president of Sports Etcetera, Ella promotes national sports and entertainment events and is partially responsible for the growing popularity of women's tennis.

Ella grew up in New York City during the 1940s and 1950s. After graduating from high school, she decided against going to college because she was most interested in the business world. While searching newspaper want ads for a job, Ella noticed an opening for a position with the Atomic Energy Commission in New York City. Instead of telephoning or writing the agency, she sent a telegram, explaining that the commission *needed* her for the job.

Ella admits she sent the telegram without having the slightest idea about what kind of job it was or whether she had the skills that were needed. But she had already developed enough self-confidence to take this type of risk. The telegram worked, and the Atomic Energy Commission gave her the job, which involved clerical and administrative work. This unusually aggressive approach to finding employment in 1959 was typical of the creativity Ella would display throughout her life.

Her advice to prospective job hunters is, "Tell them you can do whatever they need—and then do it!"

Soon after taking this new position, Ella realized she did not want to spend the rest of her life working for the federal government. She found the job too routine, with little opportunity for creativity or to be rewarded for especially good individual performance.

Seeking a greater challenge, Ella left the Atomic Energy Commission in 1962 for a job at De La Rue Bank Note Company, a British printing business (with offices in New York City) that specialized in printing stock certificates, bonds, and money for foreign countries. Part of her new job involved working in sales and calling on prospective customers to ask them for their printing jobs. From these contacts, Ella became known to many key executives in several other businesses. She also gained invaluable experience in dealing with powerful executives, which gave her the added confidence that would later help when she started her own business. Her clients were often tough and demanding. They insisted that work be done quickly, and they did not tolerate mistakes. But Ella succeeded and developed a reputation for coming through with what she had promised.

During the late 1960s, when the company decided to move its operations back to Great Britain, Ella went to U.S. Banknote, a firm that printed foreign money and U.S. food stamps. In 1969, Bill Talbert, a senior vice-president at the company, recognized that her aptitude for organization and creativity would be useful to him in a project he was working on in his free time. Bill, a famous former professional tennis champion, was in charge of the largest tennis tournament in the nation, the U.S. Open Tennis Championships, which was then played in Forest Hills, New York.

Bill realized Ella knew almost nothing about tennis, but he was impressed with her organizational skills and ideas, and asked her to help him run the U.S. Open. Years later, Ella said, "When Bill Talbert and I got together, I didn't even know how to score the game, but I was fascinated by the business challenge."

In 1969, the Open was not even close to the huge event that it is today, and the U.S. Tennis Association, which put on the event, had not been able to generate much excitement over it. There was no television coverage, no corporate sponsorship, and the prize money was $100,000, a small sum by today's standards.

Ella volunteered to help Bill with the tournament in addition to her regular duties at U.S. Banknote. "We were almost all volunteers," she said recently. "Nobody got paid." Ella immediately began to think about how to make the event bigger and better. She realized that to make the tournament more popular, they needed to attract the world's best players, including professionals. The way to do this, she reasoned, was to keep the Open a major event where both amateurs and pros could compete; to do this, prize money would have to be increased.

Left-handed tennis star Martina Navratilova dominated her sport during the 1980s, when she won the U.S. Open four times and Wimbledon each year from 1982 to 1987.

As she planned for the 1970 U.S. Open, Ella devised a new strategy for the tournament. She decided to seek corporate sponsorship of the events. After providing a certain "sponsorship fee," each corporation would receive publicity by having its name connected with the event, as well as other benefits, like tickets and hospitality for their guests. Corporate funding would also give the tournament enough money to pay for the cost of holding the tourney and perhaps make some profit.

Although corporate funding of tennis is common today, it was a new idea when Ella helped to plan the U.S. Open in 1970. The idea for corporate sponsorship provided tennis with the money needed to put the sport into the category of major sports entertainment. (Today's U.S. Open makes enough money from ticket sales and corporate sponsorships to pay for all of the costs of the U.S. junior tennis program.)

Recognizing her success with the U.S. Open, World Team Tennis asked Ella to become general manager of a team called the New York Apples in 1977. In this job, Ella continued to develop her management skills. She also learned that during a live event, anything can happen.

At a match during the summer of 1977, a city-wide blackout left 9 million New Yorkers without electricity. The lights in the arena where the tennis match was being played also went off, and 3,500 fans were left in total darkness, confused and frightened.

Ella quickly took charge. She arranged a party at the restaurant next door, and with a bullhorn she announced that tennis fans left in the auditorium were invited. Somehow, she managed to gather enough candles to provide intimate lighting and turned the evening into an unforgettable occasion.

By 1978, World Team Tennis was experiencing financial difficulties, and the New York Apples folded in

Basketball and hockey games, as well as tennis matches and many other sporting events, are held at New York City's Madison Square Garden, one of the most famous arenas in the world.

1979, leaving Ella out of a job. Days later, executives at Madison Square Garden contacted her about taking charge of what was then called the Avon Championships. The event was later known as the Virginia Slims Women's Championships and is now the Women's Tennis Association (WTA) Tour Championships. Within a week, she was in her new job. (Avon Products is one of the nation's largest manufacturers of cosmetics and women's accessories; Virginia Slims is a brand of cigarette marketed specifically for women; and the WTA is the governing body of women's tennis.)

Ella went into partnership with a former co-worker at World Team Tennis, Bill Goldstein, and together they made the Avon Championships the biggest event in women's tennis. One of her first accomplishments was getting the prize money raised to $500,000. This amount of money attracted the best tennis players, which in turn made the tournament attractive to ticket buyers.

The company that Ella and Bill established was one of the first of its kind in the United States. Named Sports Etcetera, it promotes the championships and also represents corporate clients who are interested in sponsoring events of all kinds, from sports and entertainment to cultural and charity events. Part of Ella's responsibilities as president of the company is to serve as tournament director for the Championships, which remains one of the most prestigious events in women's sports.

Ella Musolino-Alber, along with her partner Bill Goldstein, has turned women's professional tennis into a highly popular—and profitable—sport.

The Championships, as it is called, includes the top 16 singles and 8 doubles players in the world. It is the last event of the year and concludes the year-long tour that begins each January and continues through November. Players build up points throughout the season, and the player with the most points at the end of the

*The WTA Tour Championships attracts large
audiences every year.*

Championships will be named the number-one player of the year.

Sports Etcetera's responsibilities for the tournament include selling tickets, handling corporate sponsorships, and creating public awareness of the event through advertising and public relations. As tournament director, Ella is responsible for every detail of the year-ending Championships, even for selecting the music that will be played at the event. She works to see that nothing goes wrong, because lack of attention to even the smallest detail could ruin the entire event.

A problem typical of those Ella may face in her job happened a few years ago at the Championships. Before play started, she and her assistants were opening cans of tennis balls. For some unexplained reason, most of the balls were soft—"like mush," Ella said—and were unfit for use in the tourney. Ella had to scramble to locate enough good balls. From that experience and others like it, she learned always to expect the unexpected. Now she orders as many as 40 cases of brand new balls for a tournament.

As part of the promotional activities for the event, Ella provides series ticket holders with a quarterly newsletter, T-shirts, and other mementos. Weekly attendance at the first tourney in 1980 was 50,000. By 1990, attendance had doubled to 100,000, and it continues to increase each year. About 65 percent of those attending

Ella Musolino-Alber congratulates tennis players Gabriela Sabatini (left) and Arantxa Sanchez Vicario (right), pictured here with their awards.

are repeat customers. This loyal following is a testimony to the event that Ella has so effectively directed.

Since 1979, Sports Etcetera has taken on many clients and has become involved in several different kinds of events, both in sports and in other entertainment areas, such as symphonic, operatic, and dance performances. Some of their non-sporting events have been for the Merrill Lynch brokerage firm, the Met Life insurance firm, the Lipton Tea Company, and the men's fragrance Brut from Fabergé. She and her partner also work with large foundations "that are always being asked to give money to a specific cause." Ella is proud that whatever company she and Goldstein work with, they always make sure their clients get the "maximum benefit for every single dollar they spend."

Although attendance at Madison Square Garden has grown each year for women's tennis, Ella is still not satisfied. She wants "every seat filled every day" and says she "won't be happy until that happens."

The Championships is by far the biggest women's-only tennis tournament in the world, and Ella is so closely identified with it that tennis fans call it "the party that Ella throws." Every year before the tourney at Madison Square Garden, she receives flowers from many people wishing success for "her" tournament. Ella plays such a key part in the event that she moves from her regular office to an office in the Garden for the week to be close to the center of action.

Ella Musolino-Alber (second from right) with tennis champions Monica Seles, Martina Navratilova, and Steffi Graf

Ella has taken the Championships from a small regional event to a huge international success that entertains millions of people. Prize money is now up to $2 million. Because the tourney runs so smoothly, it might look like it's easy to manage. But that is only because of Ella's superb organizational ability. In spite of all the apparent confusion in putting on a big-time tennis tournament, Ella has earned a reputation for handling problems with ease. One of her employees has jokingly said, "She's so calm all the time, it's a killer. After a while, it gets contagious." For example, when Chris Evert, one of the world's best-known players, defaulted the night before the third-place playoff during a tournament in the 1980s, Ella arranged for star Pam Shriver to take Evert's place.

Ella lights up when talking about what women can accomplish in today's business world. "The opportunities for women are without limit," she has said. She explains her own success this way: "I always have to have goals, a new challenge. If I didn't have that, I don't think I could be as creative and stimulated."

Has she been a success? In the tough world of professional sports, the business part of which has long been dominated by men, Ella has made her mark. "My record speaks for itself," she responds with a smile and considerable satisfaction.

An experience during her childhood prompted Louise Woerner to build a company that provides health-care assistance to the elderly.

6

Louise Woerner
Health Care Hero

*W*hen Louise Woerner was a young girl growing up in Rochester, New York, she once saw a woman around age 50 standing on a cold street corner waiting for a bus. Louise was so affected by the sight of the woman, who looked poor and ill, that she made up her mind she would never find herself in such a situation. Years later, she admitted the fear she felt that day had motivated her to succeed.

While Louise was in high school, she worked part time at a company that published law books. One of the people she worked for, a manager named Emma Towne, would become a client of her former employee years later, after Louise had established a company to provide services for the elderly and people with disabilities so they could continue to live in their own homes.

When Louise graduated from high school in 1960, her classmates voted her "most likely to succeed." Although she received a scholarship to attend Trinity

High school student Louise Woerner solves a problem on the blackboard in her advanced placement chemistry class.

To supplement her college scholarship, Louise Woerner worked as a dorm officer at Trinity University in San Antonio.

University in San Antonio, Texas, she still had to work at various jobs during school to help pay for her expenses, such as clothes and travel to visit her family.

After graduating with high honors, Louise wanted to apply to Harvard University to earn a master's degree in business administration (MBA). However, Harvard did not accept women at that time, so she enrolled in the MBA program at the University of Chicago instead. She graduated in 1965, one of the few women in the prestigious program.

In the 1960s, women faced many obstacles in attempting to break into the business world. Newspaper want ads often specified whether a company wanted to hire a man or a woman. No matter how highly educated they were, most women were limited to jobs as secretaries, receptionists, or office assistants. Seldom were women given the opportunity to serve in an executive or management position in a large company. Both women and businesses suffered from this unfair situation. Women missed the chance to use many of their skills, and corporations missed the opportunity to gain from women's talents and good ideas.

Following graduation, many of Louise's former male classmates from the University of Chicago moved into good positions, often with large companies around the United States. Woerner's job search, however, was less successful. After spending several days interviewing for a management position with a New York firm, she was finally informed by one of the managers that the company "just isn't ready to hire a woman" for a management position—no matter how qualified she might be. Although angered and frustrated, Woerner could do little to change the employment situation. She could only find a job at which she could work as diligently and as intelligently as possible.

After getting a low-paying job at a consulting firm in Dallas, Texas, Woerner did land a succession of more rewarding jobs. She was the director of communications for the Memphis Area Chamber of Commerce in Tennessee during the late 1960s and moved to Washington, D.C., in 1970 to conduct economic analyses of community projects for the Executive Office of the President of the United States. That position helped her to secure employment as a vice-president at a Washington, D.C., management consulting firm, where she worked until 1978. Woerner later said that as a consultant, "I was an expert advising other people" before she had any actual business experience herself.

At her work, Woerner became aware of the increasing involvement of women in the work place and the demands on families. This led her to conclude that many of the tasks traditionally performed by women would simply go undone if there was no way to acquire these services from another source.

Studying the situation, Woerner found one small region of the United States that had become a leader in health care. That area was Monroe County in New York state, which was where her hometown of Rochester was located. Frustrated by the problems she saw with the lack of in-home services for the elderly, and seeing the opportunity that Monroe County provided, Woerner returned to Rochester in 1978 to start her own home care business.

At a time when few citizens were particularly aware of home care issues, Woerner had a truly innovative idea. She would provide the elderly with basic non-medical services, such as preparing their meals, helping them to bathe and dress, and caring for them following surgery. Families needing these services would pay Woerner's company to provide them.

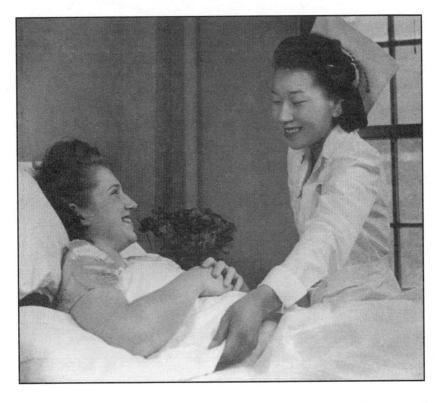

Access to high-quality health care remains a growing concern for many people, especially the elderly.

Before Woerner began her home care program, the only options available to most elderly people were to move in with their children or to have other family members care for them. But society was changing now, and family members were less available to help out than they had been in previous generations.

In 1978, Louise started HomeCare (HCR) to provide essential health care services for the elderly in their homes. At the beginning, she faced numerous financial challenges. Unable to get a bank loan, she had to charge her office furniture on her credit card. When she opened her company, her first employee earned about $300 a week, but the business often did not have enough money to pay even that amount. She frequently paid the employee out of her own salary.

Louise's first client was her former supervisor, Emma Towne, who wanted to live by herself and be as independent as possible. Although she was no longer able to run her home by herself, she wanted to age in comfort and dignity and feared that in a nursing home she would lose her independence and control. Louise's company would help this woman by coming into her home to assist with her housekeeping and personal chores.

In the late 1970s, the idea of someone actually coming into the home to help out with personal service was unusual. Louise knew that her employees had to be well trained and able to fit in with the personality of the client, so she worked hard to find and keep the right people.

Early in her career, Louise Woerner (right) speaks with Texas judge Sarah T. Hughes at a meeting of the Texas Business Leaders Club.

From the beginning, HCR had its own training program. Each new employee went through 60 hours of specialized work to learn his or her new job. By the time the training was completed, Louise knew the employee very well and was able to decide how the person would best fit into her business. Many of the people she hired had previously relied on welfare benefits or other forms of public assistance. She also began to employ nurses, physical therapists, and other trained health care aides.

106

About 85 percent of her clients' health care needs did not require a physician.

HCR got its first big break when Monroe County officials offered the company a contract as a home health care provider for the county. Open 24 hours a day, seven days a week, HCR was the first company to provide coverage in places that were difficult to reach and during times other than regular business hours.

One of the biggest difficulties Louise faced in making her new business a success, however, was the entrance of New York state and the federal government into the regulation of home care services. In 1980, both New York and federal officials decided that all private home care services must be licensed. These new rules and regulations would greatly increase the cost of HCR's services. For example, one regulation required having a doctor's order before an employee could go into a private home to prepare a meal. These regulations added to the cost of training HCR employees. It also increased office paperwork and made it more difficult to clear a profit.

With all of these new regulations, Louise might have been tempted to close down her company. Instead, she made the necessary changes and, despite the added costs, continued to grow and prosper. In 1985, she applied to the state of New York to allow her company to expand into medical home health care, and HCR was given permission in 1988. (Of the 17 other companies like hers that applied for approval, the state government ranked HCR number one in quality of service.) This certification allowed HCR to submit bills for its services directly to both Medicare (a federal program that provides basic hospital insurance for Americans who are 65 years and older or who have certain disabilities) and Medicaid for the poor.

For almost 20 years, Louise Woerner has been a leader in health care issues, both nationally and internationally. In 1983, she was named the Small Business Person of New York State. Three years later, President Ronald Reagan presented her with an award for entrepreneurial excellence.

Louise Woerner addresses the audience at a 1993 business reception.

*Louise Woerner (center) and her colleagues often
make presentations to other health care professionals.*

As home and institutional health care has grown
more complicated and far-reaching, Louise has become
deeply involved in studies of Alzheimer's disease, as well as
many other lesser-known illnesses. She also serves on
several boards of directors and is a member of a number
of national and international councils. Her company
works with international businesses and health care
providers in Japan and Russia.

In May 1994, Louise was the featured speaker at a
large health care conference in Rochester, New York, for
Sigma Theta Tau, the national nursing honor society. In
that speech, she pointed out that modern society cannot

succeed without affordable, high-quality health care. She ended her speech by saying that her opinions about health care were not "based on theories, but on 30 years of business experience" and predicted that ordinary citizens of the United States, not politicians, will be the ones to repair the system.

By 1995, HCR employed more than 500 people. HCR has offices in Rochester, New York; Atlanta, Georgia; and Burlington, Vermont. Another division of the company, the HCR Consulting Group, is based in Washington, D.C. There, 40 analysts compile research about health care issues for HCR and other organizations. The group also creates posters and other anti-smoking materials for the U.S. Office on Smoking and Health.

Louise Woerner is still the chairman and owner of the company, and 25 of her first group of employees remained with the company for more than ten years. One of the reasons her employees are so loyal is because she encourages them to make suggestions on how to improve the company—and Woerner listens to them.

Today, Woerner is more active in civic affairs than she was able to be during the early years of HCR. She frequently speaks to business organizations around her state and throughout the United States. She also tries to find time for reading (especially thriller novels), watching movies (again, thrillers), and travel, including a hiking

Like Louise Woerner, many HCR clients can smile because of the fine care her company provides.

trip to New Zealand. "I like to do things that are physically tiring," she has said. "It's good for balance."

Women have come a long way since the days when Louise Woerner could not find a job to match her skills in a male-dominated business world. When asked about the possibilities for women in business today, she sums up her experiences this way:

> Maybe it wasn't smart, but I always felt I had to be the first one with a new business idea. The easy way would have been to let some big company do it. But I was willing to stick my neck out and take a gamble. Maybe that's entrepreneurship. It's like being at the top of a five-story roller coaster and looking down. The uncertainty is part of the fun!

As president of the ARCHI-FORM commercial design firm, Masako Boissonnault has turned her childhood ambition into a reality.

7

Masako Boissonnault
Thriving by Design

*M*asako Boissonnault is the founder and head of her own interior design firm in Los Angeles, California. Her company, called ARCHI-FORM, has as its clients large and small companies throughout the United States, Canada, and Japan.

Masako Tani was born in Tokyo, in 1944, a year before the end of World War II. After losing the war, Japan slowly began to change from a traditional culture to a modern society. Many observers have noted that Japan would change more in the ten years after World War II than any time in its history.

Masako's father, Hiroyoshi Tani, owned a small business in Tokyo that made *kimonos*, the traditional loose robes with wide sleeves and a sash at the waist that Japanese women wear as an outer garment. Her father had lost the business during the war, but he started it up again in late 1945 when the fighting was over. Masako was the youngest in her family; she had four older sisters and an older brother. Her parents expected their children not only to help at home, but also to work with them in their kimono business. Because it was customary for the oldest son to enter the family business, Masako's brother did so, even though he had wanted to study to become an architect.

Although Masako's father had no formal education, he understood the need for learning and encouraged his children to work hard in school. In addition to attending academic classes, Masako took drawing lessons. She also learned to play the piano and to dance. Like many other Japanese men at that time, however, her father felt that women should be kept "in their place." He often told her that "the smartest woman is equal to the dumbest man," a point of view that did little to instill self-confidence in the young girl. But when her mother, Katu Tani, died, 13-year-old Masako was forced to become more self-sufficient and take over many of the household responsibilities.

By the late 1950s, when Masako was in high school, her older sisters had all married. For some time, she had dreamed of becoming a commercial designer—someone who would, for example, decorate a business office by selecting furniture, accessories, and floor and wall coverings. To learn as much as she could about art and design, Masako went to a college in Tokyo and graduated with a degree in fine art. Because women in Japan had few opportunities to excel in the work force, Masako decided to move to the United States. She believed that businesses there would be more receptive to women than they were in Japan.

To prepare herself for life in the United States, Masako studied English for nearly two years before leaving Japan. When she felt confident enough in her ability to communicate in the language of her new country, Masako applied for entrance to the Arts Center College of Los Angeles. After learning she had been accepted into college, she had to convince her father and the rest of her family that leaving her native country was the right decision for her.

Masako finally left Japan in 1969, and began her studies in Los Angeles later that year. She told herself that if she did not do well in school, she would return to Japan. In an interview years later, she explained how the challenge of moving to a new country helped to motivate her to succeed:

There are many remarkable opportunities in the American free enterprise system—especially for women. When you are forced to survive on your own in a new country, without family and friends, you learn very quickly about your strengths and your weaknesses. I strongly believe you must have patience, because success takes time.

In 1973, with her design studies completed, Masako began working at Kajima International, a Japanese-owned design firm with offices in Los Angeles. There, she worked on interior design projects for banks, restaurants, hotels, and office buildings. After nearly five years at Kajima, she left the company and began a career as a freelance design consultant. Now she was essentially her own boss, advising customers about business design problems they were not able to solve by themselves. In this new work, she dealt mostly with Japanese-Americans. Before long, however, she realized that if she were to be truly successful, she must broaden her base of clients.

Joining an American-owned firm offered Masako a wider range of more complicated design projects. She also began learning about business management and finance, as well as long-term planning, promotion, marketing, and public relations. These were all skills she would need to have should she ever start her own business. By the late 1970s, Masako Tani's name was well known in the design industry in California. She had

Masako Boissonnault discusses various fabric designs with a client.

earned a reputation as someone who did excellent work and completed projects on time or ahead of schedule.

During her student days at the Arts Center College, Masako had met Neil Boissonnault, a French-Canadian who was working in Los Angeles. They were married in 1972. Neil believed in his wife's talents and encouraged her to start her own business. She agreed and, with a $5,000 loan from friends, established an architectural and design firm, ARCHI-FORM, later that year with her

Masako Boissonnault uses illustrations to present ideas to her clients.

partner, Jerry Lomas. Masako's first client was Citicorp, a large banking and financial service that owned a nationally known credit card company, Carte Blanche. Citicorp hired her to design the interior of Carte Blanche's headquarters.

After completing the Carte Blanche offices, Masako had enough money to pay off her loan and spend time securing other clients. Soon she had added several banks in the Los Angeles area to her client list. She also began to do design work for restaurants and hotels. Another well-known credit card company, Diner's Club, became her client, as did Mattel, a large toy company. She now began to spend much of her time designing textiles to use in the offices of her many business clients, and soon her fabrics were being sold throughout the United States and Canada, as well as in her native Japan.

Eventually, Masako became so well known and successful that, in 1984, four years after she had founded her company, she was recognized by the American Business Women's Association as one of the year's top ten U.S. businesswomen. Two years later, President Ronald Reagan invited her to a reception for business leaders at the White House.

In the late 1980s, Masako began teaching design courses to college students and got involved in many community organizations and professional groups, including the American Business Women's Association and the National Women's Economic Alliance. She also helped others get started in business by participating in a mentoring program called the Women's Network for Entrepreneurial Training, which was sponsored by the Small Business Administration (SBA). As a mentor, she served as an informal teacher and adviser to young women who wanted to enter the business world.

In her role as mentor, Masako met a young woman named Wendy Blasdell who had started her own business creating food and table settings for movies and television programs. Although she was very good at her job,

*The offices for the Siam Commercial Bank in
Los Angeles were designed by ARCHI-FORM.*

120

she needed sound advice on bookkeeping, accounting, marketing, advertising, and other business practices.

Blasdell read an article about the SBA's mentoring program, which pairs successful women entrepreneurs with young women wishing to get started. When Blasdell wrote a letter asking for help, Masako Boissonnault was chosen to advise her. Masako's own business kept her busy, but she said, "I am in the design business, and so is she. She is very creative, and she needed help."

Masako's attitude about this reflects her total outlook on life and her spirit of helpful service. She recently said, "I am Japanese, and I have gotten a lot from living and working in this country. Now I can return something. So much has been done for me, now I can do something for someone else."

About her association with her mentor, Blasdell says, "Masako has shown me ways to get clients and how to manage my time better. She gives me inspiration and helps keep me on track. If not for this program, I really would have missed out on the value of her experience and her encouragement."

Boissonnault's advice for Blasdell—and for anyone wanting to succeed—is that people who look for success must have at least one specific goal. With that goal in mind, they must then develop habits that will help them to accomplish their goals. Boissonnault has always encouraged would-be entrepreneurs to take risks. "Above

An avid rider, Masako Boissonnault often cycles to and from her office in Los Angeles.

all," she tells prospective entrepreneurs, "don't be afraid of failure."

Still, Boissonnault cautions that a business must never become overextended. Instead, it is important for executives to limit the number of projects they select so there is enough time to give each client the best possible attention through all stages of development.

Today, Masako and her husband, Neil, live in a beautiful home in San Pedro, California, overlooking the Pacific Ocean. Here she can relax and get away from the pressures of running a demanding business. Looking at all of her achievements may lead one to assume that Boissonnault's life has been easy and that success and fame came to her without a struggle. "Not so," she says. "There *is* no short cut."

*When a hang-gliding accident left her paralyzed
from the waist down, Marilyn Hamilton decided to
design wheelchairs that people would be proud to own.*

8

Marilyn Hamilton
Winner on Wheels

*I*n the summer of 1978, a 29-year-old high school teacher named Marilyn Hamilton had a devastating hang-gliding accident in the California Sierras. Her spinal cord was severely injured in the accident, paralyzing the lower half of her body. Marilyn was now a paraplegic, and her doctors told her she would never walk again.

This accident could have destroyed Marilyn, who had led a very active life. But it did not, because she was not willing to accept the idea that a wheelchair was a prison. What she did do, not only for herself, but also for

Marilyn Hamilton at Motion Designs, which has won national attention for manufacturing wheelchairs that are faster, lighter, and more maneuverable than earlier models.

every other person living with lower body paralysis, was to start a company to improve the quality of wheelchairs and reduce the stigma of using them.

Marilyn's uncle, Bill Hamilton, also used a wheelchair. Bill had been thrown from a car when he was young, and the accident left him a quadriplegic, unable to move his arms or legs. Soon after Marilyn's accident, her uncle came to the hospital to see her. From his experience of 50 years as a quadriplegic, he spoke to Marilyn reassuringly. "You can do anything," he told her. "You're bright. You're adventurous. Don't let that spirit die."

In the late 1920s, when Bill Hamilton had been injured, wheelchairs were clumsy and poorly designed. Made of wood and wicker, the chairs were heavy and rigid, which made them difficult to maneuver. They were also too wide to go through most doors.

Furthermore, wheelchairs at that time did not have motors, so someone had to push a paralyzed person's wheelchair. (Bill's first wheelchair, for example, weighed about 90 pounds. He had two attendants who stayed with him 24 hours a day and accompanied him to class when he attended college and law school.)

During the 1930s, the Everest & Jennings company designed a wheelchair that weighed only 50 pounds. However, few improvements had been made in wheelchair design since that time. It was partly for that reason that many people, especially employers, looked upon disabled people in chairs as useless and believed wheelchairs were only for people confined forever to their own home or to an institution.

Prior to her accident, Marilyn—who was born on March 30, 1949—had enjoyed a life filled with promise. After receiving a bachelor's degree in home economics from California State Polytechnic University, she began teaching high school in 1972 and had spent two years teaching in Australia. She had enjoyed skiing, sailing, and tennis.

The days following Marilyn's accident were extremely difficult for her. Although her drive and competitive spirit got her through rehabilitation in just three weeks (instead of the months it usually took), she had trouble accepting that she would never walk again. At this time, Marilyn decided to leave the high school in Kingsburg, California, where she had taught home economics for four years. Instead, she took on the challenge of working as a broker for her uncle Bill at L. R. Hamilton, the family's fruit business in Reedley, California, where they grew, packed, and shipped fruit worldwide.

Marilyn was not happy with her first wheelchair, which she referred to as a "stainless steel dinosaur." Although the chair was the best available in 1978, she found it difficult to maneuver. From the moment she got into the chair, Marilyn noticed the way people, even friends and relatives, acted around her. "I was the same person I had always been," she later said, "but people were scared and nervous in the presence of the chair."

Her friends were awkward and didn't know what to say or how to act. Doctors tended to speak to Marilyn's family instead of to her, although she would be sitting directly in front of them. When her friends came to her home, they were so sad she had to cheer them up instead of the other way around.

Because she did not want people to feel sorry for her simply because she used a wheelchair, Marilyn decided she would change the public's feelings about wheelchairs and the people who used them. She wanted people to know that just because you are in a wheelchair, you're not an invalid or a sick person who wants pity. As she viewed the situation, a person in a wheelchair simply moved about in a different way from others. Although she acknowledged that people who used wheelchairs couldn't do everything that others could, one of her personal mottos became, "If you can't stand up, stand out!"

Marilyn had previously flown hang-gliders with two friends who were engineers, Don Helman and Jim Okamoto. Now she contacted them to help her design a new type of wheelchair to improve peoples' lives with state-of-the-art technology. She thought chairs should be both easy to use and attractive to the eye—creating function, freedom, and fun while providing dignity. Instead of the usual chrome color, she wanted to offer chairs in exciting, energetic colors like canary yellow, apple red, electric green, and even bright pink. Marilyn wanted

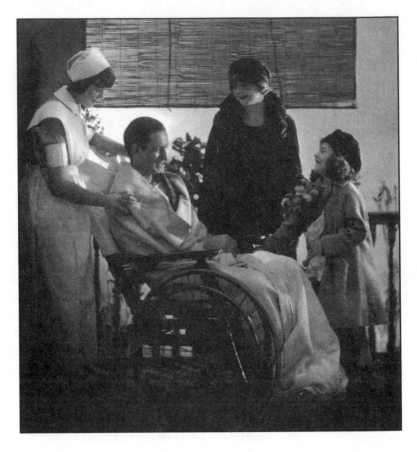

During much of the twentieth century, many people thought that wheelchair users were almost helpless and needed special attention.

people to be proud of their wheelchairs, just like people are proud of their cars.

The wheelchair that Marilyn, Don, and Jim built in 1980 was a vast improvement over the models that had been used for decades. Constructed from aluminum tubing (as hang gliders are), the new wheelchair weighed only 26 pounds—about half as much as traditional chairs in 1978. Its low back gave it a sporty look, and the adjustable frame was far more compact and lightweight than earlier models, providing high performance. These modifications and the ability to customize a chair to an individual's needs and wants would contribute greatly to the quality of life for hundreds of thousands of people who spend their lives in chairs.

In 1980, Marilyn and her two partners established a company, Motion Designs, to manufacture their new chair, which they named the "Quickie." They began selling their new wheelchairs almost as fast as they could build them. The company's slogan is "Get Out There" and they have used such inspiring mottos as "Wheels for Winners" and "No Limit" over the past 15 years. In their promotional materials, they wrote the word "disabled" as "disAbled" to emphasize that using a wheelchair does not define or completely limit someone. The company soon diversified its product line, manufacturing many specialized chairs, including the easily adjustable Quickie Recliner, the Quickie Kidz for toddlers, and the Quickie Folding wheelchair. In 1993, Quickie launched a revolutionary power wheelchair called the P200. *Popular Mechanics* magazine dubbed the P200 the "Ferrari of wheelchairs" because at seven MPH it could travel more than 25 percent faster than other powered chairs.

During the early 1960s, nearly 20 years before Marilyn's accident, many people had begun to change the way they thought about individuals in wheelchairs. At that time, more than 500,000 Americans were using chairs, and journalists began writing about the growing number of people with disabilities. In the late 1960s and early 1970s, thousands of men returning to the United States had to use wheelchairs because of injuries they sustained during the Vietnam War. In the years following the war, wheelchair users began to speak up, asking to have curbings on street corners cut down to permit them to cross streets freely. They also requested lifts on buses and specially designed cars, as well as designated parking places.

As the U.S. awakened to the needs of people with disabilities, architects began to design restrooms in public buildings so that wheelchair users could get in and out of the toilet stalls in their chairs. The federal government passed laws that gave disabled persons the opportunity to attend college, secure employment, and live lives as close to normal as anyone else. Today, approximately 1.5 million people in the United States use wheelchairs, and most of them live in their own homes. Because of recent improvements in medical technology and public accommodations, people who use wheelchairs now have a far better chance to lead comfortable and productive lives than they did 20 years ago. It was into this new understanding of the problems of wheelchair users that Marilyn Hamilton came with her brightly colored chairs.

The Quickie's performance not only made it easier for users to become more mobile in their daily lives, but also to participate in athletic events. Marilyn herself began competing internationally in tennis and snow skiing, and when other athletes who used wheelchairs saw the Quickie's performance at these sporting events, they wanted to buy her chair. Marilyn went on to become a two-time national wheelchair tennis champion. And as a ten-year member of the U.S. Disabled Ski Team, Marilyn was a Paralympic ski champion twice, and a National Champion six times. She was also inducted into the California Governor's Hall of Fame for People with Disabilities.

In 1985, yearly sales for Motion Designs soared to $15 million. The business employed about 200 people and had twice relocated to larger locations. That year, Marilyn was also named California Business Woman of the Year.

Marilyn and her partners, after seven years of phenomenal growth, decided in December, 1986, that they wanted to merge with a larger organization that could provide the sophisticated management expertise a worldwide, fast-growth company needed. It was becoming increasingly difficult to build the infrastructure necessary to support Motion Designs's rapid growth. The partners found a perfect fit with Sunrise Medical, the leading home health care manufacturer worldwide and a company dedicated to improving the quality of people's

Marilyn Hamilton meets with Vice-President Dan
Quayle at the White House in 1992.

lives through its products and services. Their division
became Quickie Designs, Inc. and Marilyn became the
first Senior Vice President of Marketing and then, in
1994, she was promoted to Vice President of Corporate
Responsibility at Sunrise Medical.

Today, Marilyn reflects that Quickie's success has
come from innovation, high quality products, empow-
ered associates, taking risks, and having fun. Quickie
employees see opportunities instead of problems. Thus,
they find creative solutions. One example of Quickie's
desire to serve its clients better is its promise to fill all

orders for wheelchairs within 21 days. Also, people with disabilities who use chairs are an active part of the Quickie work force, which includes a large percentage of women and minorities. Currently, Quickie Designs accounts for approximately 20 percent of Sunrise Medical's annual sales.

As part of Quickie's marketing program, Marilyn sponsors athletes who use wheelchairs to compete in a variety of athletic events, including tennis, basketball, skiing, and track and field. Dave Kiley and Randy Snow are two of the well-known Paralympic athletes who have helped promote Quickie's wheelchairs. Snow is a ten-time U.S.

Marilyn Hamilton, with former Paralympic athletes Skip Wilkins (left) and wheelchair basketball player and skier David Kiley.

In 1990, Marilyn Hamilton is honored at Dodger Stadium in Los Angeles for her outstanding work for disabled people.

Open Wheelchair Tennis champion and Kiley is a Paralympic Champion in both basketball and snow skiing.

Sunrise Medical is an official sponsor of the 1996 Atlanta Paralympic Games, the world's second largest sporting event next to the Olympic games. More than 4,000 athletes from 110 countries will come to Georgia to compete in at least 19 different events. Sunrise Medical also sponsors many of the teams and athletes worldwide who will be competing in the Paralympics.

In April, 1991, Marilyn created and launched with Sunrise Medical as its founding partner an innovative non-profit program called Winners on Wheels, informally called WOW. WOW is a growing national network of community based programs designed to advance the leadership of children and youth with disabilities. WOW has created magic in the lives of children who use wheelchairs through innovative life-experience programs designed to enhance self-esteem, promote achievement, emphasize fun, increase independence, and develop teamwork. Nationwide, there are over 400 children participating through 41 local circles that are supported by committed volunteer leaders and a small national staff headquartered in Fresno, California. When asked about her philosophy of life, Marilyn smiles and answers, "My life has been wonderful, not always easy, but full of new adventures." She adds:

> My favorite saying is I am not made—or unmade—by the things that happen to me, but instead, how I react to them. With the right attitude, life is full of possibilities and opportunities. If you build a dream, the dream will build you.

About her future, Marilyn says, "The sky is the limit. In fact, there is no limit."

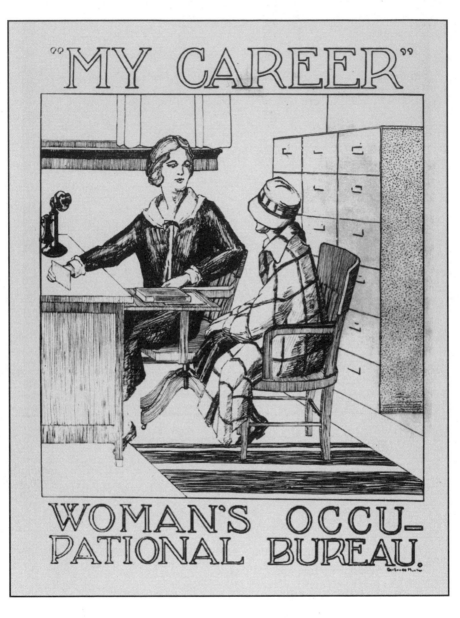

This poster from 1925 for the Women's Occupational Bureau shows how women began to think about having a career during the early part of the twentieth century.

More Notable Twentieth-Century Businesswomen

In addition to the eight women profiled in this book, numerous other women have run companies successfully. Some of these women are listed in alphabetical order below:

- Anderson, Margaret Caroline. b. 1893? in Indianapolis, Ind. In 1914, founded and became editor of the *Little Review*, a prestigious magazine about the arts. d. 1973.

- Arden, Elizabeth. b. 1884 in Woodbridge, Ontario, Canada. In 1915, began marketing an internationally successful line of cosmetics. Operated more than 100 beauty salons across Europe for elite clientele. d. 1966.

- Auerbach, Beatrice Fox. b. 1887 in Hartford, Conn. President of Fox & Company, one of the nation's largest privately owned department stores, from 1938 to 1965. d. 1968.

- Bay, Josephine Holt Perfect. b. 1900 in Anamosa, Iowa. Ran a successful Christmas card business with her sister, then succeeded her husband as director of American Export Lines, a major shipping firm. She was the first woman to head a member firm of the New York Stock Exchange. d. 1962.

- Beech, Olive Ann. b. 1903 in Waverly, Kans. Converted a small airplane operation into a major contractor for the U.S. Department of Defense.

- Bishop, Hazel Gladys. b. 1906 in Hoboken, N.J. Formed Hazel Bishop, Inc., in 1950 to manufacture "Lasting Lipstick" and other cosmetics. Became a registered agent for the Bache and Company brokerage firm in 1962.

- Carnegie, Hattie. b. 1886? in Vienna, Austria. In 1913, co-founded a business, (later called Hattie Carnegie, Inc.) that manufactured and sold fashionable clothing. d. 1956.

- Cochran, Jacqueline. b. 1910? in Pensacola, Fla. A highly skilled aviator who founded a prosperous cosmetics business in 1934. d. 1980.

- Fields, Debbi. b. 1956 in East Oakland, Calif. During the early 1980s, opened the first outlet of Mrs. Fields Cookies, which sells baked desserts nationally.

- Frederick, Christine McGaffey. b. 1883 in Boston, Mass. In 1910, founded the Apple Croft Home Experiment Station, which tested household appliances and products. Founded the League of Advertising Women in 1912. d. 1970.

- Gleason, Kate. b. 1865 in Rochester, N.Y. Chief sales representative for her father's toolmaking business. The first woman named to the American Society of Engineers. Acted as president of the First National Bank of East Rochester from 1917 to 1919. d. 1933.

- Graham, Bette Nesmith. b.1924 in Dallas, Tex. A secretary who invented and began manufacturing Liquid Paper in 1956. d. 1980.

- Graham, Katharine Meyer. b. 1917 in New York, N.Y. Became president and publisher of the highly successful *Washington Post* newspaper during the 1960s.

- Green, Hetty. b. 1834 in New Bedford, Mass. Made $100 million as a financial investor on Wall Street. d. 1916.

Secretary Bette Nesmith Graham designed Liquid Paper to "white out" her typing mistakes—and millions of students and office workers are grateful for her invention.

- Grossinger, Jennie. b. 1892 in Baligrod, Austria. Managed prestigious hotels and resorts for several decades. d. 1972.

- Handler, Ruth. b. 1916 in Denver, Colo. Co-founded Mattel Toys in 1944 and created the popular Barbie doll.

- Hawes, Elizabeth. b. 1903 in Ridgewood, N.J. In 1928, co-founded an internationally known fashion-designing business, later called Hawes, Inc. d. 1971.

Ruth Handler, who founded Mattel Toys with her husband and another business partner, named the Barbie doll after her daughter. (The Ken doll was named for her son.)

General Mills's fictional character, Betty Crocker, shown here in 1950, has changed with the times—just as American attitudes toward women have changed.

• Husted, Marjorie Child. b. 1892? in Minneapolis, Minn. In 1929, became director of the Betty Crocker Homemaking Service, a department of General Mills. d. 1986

• Jones, Mary Harris (better known as "Mother Jones"). b. 1830 in Cork, Ireland. Operated a dress-making business in Chicago, but became nationally known as a labor organizer from the 1870s until her death. d. 1930.

• Katz, Lillian. b. 1927 in Leipzig, Germany. Chief executive officer of the Lillian Vernon corporation, the mail order business which she created in 1950.

• Klein, Anne. b. 1923 in Brooklyn, N.Y. Started her own manufacturing company, Anne Klein and Co. d. 1974.

143

- Knox, Rose Markward. b. 1857 in Mansfield, Ohio. Co-founded the Knox Gelatin Company in 1890. Became the first woman member of the American Grocery Manufacturers' Association. d. 1950.

- Muller, Gertrude Agnes. b. 1887 in Leo, Ind. In 1924, founded Juvenile Wood Products Company (later Toidey Company), to manufacture child-safety products. d. 1957.

- Patterson, Alicia. b. 1906 in Chicago, Ill. Publisher and editor of the successful daily newspaper, *Newsday*, from 1940 until her death. d. 1963.

- Roddick, Anita. b. 1942 in Littlehampton, England. In 1976, opened the Body Shop, which manufactures and sells cosmetics made from natural products.

- Rosenberg, Anna Marie. b. 1902 in Budapest, Austria-Hungary. Opened a consulting firm in 1924 to assist large companies with labor relations. Became an adviser to President Franklin D. Roosevelt.

- Rosenthal, Ida Cohen. b. 1886 in Rakov, Russia. Opened a successful dressmaking business, which eventually became Maiden Form, Inc. d. 1973.

- Rubinstein, Helena. b. 1871 in Kraków, Poland (then part of Austria). Developed a successful line of cosmetics and operated beauty salons in Europe and the United States. d. 1965.

- Rudkin, Margaret Fogarty. b. 1897 in New York, N.Y. Founded the Pepperidge Farm bakeries in 1937. d. 1967.

• Schiff, Dorothy. b. 1903 in New York, N.Y. President and publisher of the *New York Post* newspaper. d. 1989.

• Shaver, Dorothy. b. 1897 in Center Point, Ark. In 1945, became president of Lord & Taylor, a famous Fifth Avenue specialty store. d. 1959.

• Steinem, Gloria. b. 1934 in Toledo, Ohio. In 1972, became the founding editor of *Ms.* magazine. Sold the business in 1987.

The January 1973 issue of Ms. *magazine had a cover story about politicians Frances Farenthold and Shirley Chisholm. Like* Ms. *founder Gloria Steinem, many women throughout U.S. history have become publishers.*

Today, Totino's frozen pizza remains a popular item at grocery stores.

- Totino, Rose. b. 1915 in Minneapolis, Minn. In 1951, co-founded a frozen pizza company and later became a vice-president at the Pillsbury Company. d. 1994.

- Trigère, Pauline. b. 1912 in Paris, France. Established Trigère, Inc., a New York City fashion-design firm, in 1942.

- Walker, Maggie Lena. b. 1867 in Richmond, Va. In 1903, opened the St. Luke Penny Savings Bank, which later bought out several other firms to become the Consolidated Bank and Trust Company during the 1930s. d. 1934.

- Walker, Sarah Breedlove. b. 1867 near Delta, La. Owned and operated the Madam C.J. Walker Manufacturing Company, which produced a line of hair-care products for black women. Became the first African-American woman millionaire. d. 1919.

- Wells, Mary Georgene. b. 1928 in Youngstown, Ohio. Along with two business partners, established Wells, Rich, Greene, Inc., one of Madison Avenue's most successful advertising agencies, in 1966.

- White, Eartha M. Magdalene. b. 1876 in Jacksonville, Fla. A political activist and entrepreneur who operated several small businesses—and then sold them each for a profit. d. 1974.

The success of Wonderful Hair Grower and other products helped to turn businesswoman C.J. Walker into a millionaire.

Bibliography

Ash, Mary Kay. *Mary Kay.* New York: Harper and Row, 1987.

_____. *Mary Kay on People Management.* New York: Warner, 1984.

"Best Entrepreneurs, The." *Minnesota Ventures,* August 1993.

Billings, Laura. "A Taste for Business." *Minnesota Monthly,* July 1994.

Bird, Caroline. *Enterprising Women.* New York: Norton, 1976.

Boehm, Helen F., with Nancy Dunnan. *With a Little Luck: An American Odyssey.* New York: Ramson, 1985.

Cantor, Dorothy W., and Toni Bernay. *Women in Power: The Secrets of Leadership.* Boston: Houghton Mifflin, 1992.

Chandler, Cara Wommack. "The Good News Is . . . 1985." *Dallas Magazine,* December 1985.

Chin, Leeann. *Betty Crocker's Chinese Cookbook, Recipes by Leeann Chin.* New York: Random House, 1981.

Coffee, Robert, and Richard Scare. *Women in Charge: The Experience of Female Entrepreneurs.* Boston: Unwin, 1985.

Cohen, Sherry Suib. *Tender Power: A Revolutionary Approach to Work and Intimacy.* Reading, Mass.: Addison-Wesley, 1989.

Dight, Janet. *Breaking the Secretary Barrier: How to Get Out from Behind the Typewriter and Into a Management Job.* New York: McGraw Hill, 1986.

Drucker, Peter F. *Innovation and Entrepreneurship: Practice and Principles.* New York: Harper and Row, 1985.

Farnham, Alan. "Mary Kay's Lessons in Leadership." *Fortune*, September 20, 1993.

Goad, Kimberly. "Ellen Terry: A Big-Picture Window Is Realtor's Key to Success." *The Dallas Morning News*, January 23, 1994.

Hamilton, Martha B. "Women Seeking SBA Loans Wage an Up-Hill Fight." *The Washington Post*, July 14, 1981.

Hammerstrom, Grace. "Quality Assurance." *Q* magazine, November 1989.

Harrison, Patricia. *America's New Women Entrepreneurs.* Washington, D.C.: Acropolis, 1986.

Jennings, Diane. *Self-Made Women: Twelve of America's Leading Entrepreneurs Talk about Success, Self-Image, and the Superwoman.* Dallas: Taylor, 1987.

Laney, W. L. *How to Be Boss in a Hurry: A Primer for New Managers.* Indianapolis: Bobbs-Merrill, 1982.

Leavitt, Judith. *Women in Management: An Annotated Bibliography and Sourcelist.* Phoenix: Oryz, 1987.

Madden, Tara Roth. *Women vs. Women.* New York: Amacom, 1987.

Matthaei, Julie A. *An Economic History of Women in America*. New York: Schocken, 1982.

McHenry, Robert. *Famous American Women: A Biographical Dictionary from Colonial Times to the Present*. New York: Dover, 1980.

Maurer, Rick. *Caught in the Middle*. Cambridge, Mass.: Productivity Press, 1992.

Mulhern, Bill. "Ella Musolino: Co-founder and President, Sports Etcetera." *The Executive Female*, May/June 1985.

Perri, Colleen. *Entrepreneurial Women*. Kenosha, Wis.: Possibilities Publishing, 1989.

Reif, Rita. "Mrs. Boehm's Rich World of Porcelain." *The New York Times*, January 26, 1975.

Scholard, Jeannette R. *The Self-Employed Woman*. New York: Simon and Schuster, 1985.

Scoth, Mary, and Howard Rothman. *Companies with a Conscience: Intimate Portraits of Twelve Firms that Make a Difference*. New York: Carol, 1992.

Sheperd, Nina. "Journey of a Thousand Smiles." *Corporate Report Minnesota*, May 1986.

Shmerler, Cindy. "Professional's Profession." *World Tennis*, November 1986.

Sprei, Doug. "Louise Woerner: HCR's Founder Proves that the Private Sector Can Marshall Improvement in Health Care." *Rochester Business Magazine*, December 1990.

"Sunrise Medical, Inc. 1993 Annual Report." Fresno, Calif.: Sunrise Medical, Inc. 1993.

Whisler, Thomas L. *Rules of the Game.* Homewood, Ill.: Dow Jones, 1984.

Zaroff, Carolyn. "Introducing Louise Woerner." *Rochester Women*, August 1984.

Zipay, Steve. "Making the Slims into Big Business." *New York Newsday*, November 19, 1993.

Zoglin, Gilbert. G. *From Executive to Entrepreneur.* New York: Amacom, 1991.

Index

Kiley, Dave, 135-136
kiln, 41
kimonos, 114

Leeann Chin, Inc., 54, 64
Leeann Chin Carryout
    Chinese Cuisine, 60
Leeann Chin Chinese
    Cuisine, 58, 61
Lee Wai-Hing, 54. *See also*
    Chin, Leann
Lipton Tea Company, 95
Lomas, Jerry, 118
Loren, Sophia, 51
L. R. Hamilton, 128

Madison Square Garden, 83,
    89, 90, 95
Malvern, England, Boehm
    Studio in, 46, 48, 50
Mao Tse-tung, 48, 49
Mary Kay Cosmetics, 17, 21,
    22, 29, 32, 35; founding
    of, 27; incentives offered
    by, 33, 34; organization
    of, 29, 30, 32; success of,
    27, 29, 31, 35
*Mary Kay on People
    Management*, 35
Mary Kay pink, 34
Mattel, 119
Mechanical School of
    Optics, 39

Medicaid, 108
Medicare, 108
Memphis Area Chamber of
    Commerce, 103
Merrill Lynch, 95
Met Life, 95
Metropolitan Museum of
    Art, 42-43
Meyrowitz Optical Center,
    40, 44
Minneapolis, 53, 54, 57, 58,
    60, 62
Minnesota Business Hall of
    Fame, 64
Minnesota Twins, 53
Monroe County, New York,
    health care in, 103, 107
Motion Designs, 19, 126,
    131, 133
Musolino-Alber, Ella, 19, 82;
    business philosophy of,
    84-85; early years of, 84;
    as president of Sports
    Etcetera, 84, 90, 93, 95;
    work of, in organizing
    tennis tournaments, 83-
    84, 86, 88, 90-91, 93-97
"Mute Swans, Birds of
    Peace," 48, 49

National Association of
    Women Business Owners
    (NAWBO), 65

ABOUT THE AUTHOR

ROBERT PILE retired during the 1980s as senior vice president of one of the nation's largest advertising agencies. During his 40 years in the advertising business, his clients included Tonka Toys, Procter and Gamble, Pillsbury, National Car Rental, and Dairy Queen. Pile has taught advertising at the University of Minnesota and serves on the board of directors of two U.S. firms. He is the author of *Top Entrepreneurs and Their Businesses*, as well as two novels, a book about European travel, a book about entrepreneur Rose Totino, and several newspaper and magazine articles. He has six children and eight grandchildren, and he lives in Minneapolis.

Photo Credits
Photographs courtesy of Grand Metropolitan PLC, pp. 8, 146; Lindy Advertising Cuts from the 1920s and 1930s, p. 14; Library of Congress, pp. 16, 56, 104, 130; The Bettmann Archives, pp. 18, 43; Mary Kay Cosmetics, pp. 20, 25, 28, 31, 32; Girl Scout Council of Greater Minneapolis, p. 23; The Boehm Studio, pp. 36, 38 (both), 45, 47, 50, 51; Leeann Chin, Inc., pp. 52, 57, 59, 60, 62, 63, 65, 66; Ellen Terry and Ellen Terry, Realtors, pp. 68, 71, 75, 76, 79, 80; Sports Etcetera, pp. 82, 87, 89, 91, 92, 94 (both), 96; Louise Woerner and HomeCare, pp. 98, 100, 101, 106, 108, 109, 111; ARCHI-FORM, pp. 112, 117, 118, 120, 122; Quickie Designs, pp. 124, 126, 134, 135, 136; the Minnesota Historical Society, pp. 138, 143; The Gillette Co., p. 141; Mattel Inc., p. 142; and the Indiana Historical Society, p. 147;